# HAUNTED GLASGOW

Ron Halliday

Fort Publishing Ltd

First published in 2008 by Fort Publishing Ltd, Old Belmont House,
12 Robsland Avenue, Ayr KA7 2RW

Printed by Bell and Bain Ltd

Graphic design by Mark Blackadder

Cover art by Malgorzata Maj of Sarachmet Photopainting
and Retro Photography

Typeset by 3btype.com

ISBN: 978-1-905769-08-7

# Contents

# Preface

I freely admit that for a long time after I first became interested in ghosts, poltergeists, UFOs and other psychic phenomena Glasgow did not immediately strike me as the place to research the supernatural. The image of the industrial and financial giant seemed at odds with 'other worldly' aspects. If I thought of a mystic location the places that came to mind were the standing stones of Callanish, Arthur's Seat in Edinburgh or the haunted rooms of Glamis Castle. That was my view for several years. It was only as cases of supernatural phenomena occurring in the city kept coming to my attention and I developed contacts with psychics from Glasgow that it gradually dawned on me that here was a place of intense interest lying on my doorstep. A city where many strange incidents of a supernatural nature occur and have occurred stretching back across the centuries. In spite of the city's image it's amazing to think that it started life as a spiritual focus. That even before the Christian missionary St Kentigern arrived it was an area of mystic activity that attracted groups like the Druids and followers of other pagan religions who made it their home. The evidence for Glasgow's ancient spiritual origins, the reasons why it has proved attractive for a long line of mystics, has remained hidden within the buildings and the landscape that spreads out from the cathedral to the area now covered by the city centre. For the first time I have, in the pages of *Haunted Glasgow*, revealed and described the evidence for this 'secret' history of the city, which survives, unremarked, all around us. It has influenced generation after generation and given that background it is easier to understand why Glasgow can produce so many ghost, UFO, poltergeist, witchcraft and Satanism incidents. It's a hidden part of the city's history and contemporary life.

I have been researching psychic phenomena for over twenty-five years and in that time have encountered a range of supernatural events that almost defy belief. Many of these incidents I have recounted in *Haunted Glasgow*. In fact, I would say that for a city which prides itself on its pragmatic side almost everything paranormal seems to have occurred at one time or another. And this, as I detail in *Haunted Glasgow*, is not a recent development. It's the hidden side of Glasgow that rarely hits the headlines. Even the fact that the city has a long history of witchcraft activity stretching back across the centuries seems to have gone by largely unnoticed. I have covered the development of witchcraft from the past down to the present as one of the 'secret', if you like, themes of the city. But there is so much to tell, from ghosts to UFOs to poltergeists. Every area of the city seems to have experienced in one way or another supernatural incidents of some kind. Could there be an explanation for this? Invisible streams of energy known as 'ley lines' may be the source of these events, as according to some they allow ghosts, poltergeists and other phantoms to appear and can even affect your health.

In May 1997 I began the 'X-Files' column in Glasgow's *Evening Times*. It was great to have the opportunity every week over several years to write about the many kinds of paranormal incidents that had occurred in the city and had either been reported directly to me or I was aware of from past investigations. It also brought me into contact with a range of people whose experience almost defies belief, but whose tales, quietly and calmly told, in an almost matter-of-fact manner, have convinced me that we sit on the edge of a strange meeting of worlds. An interaction of dimensions that may be beyond our current understanding, but brings us, from time to time, into contact with events contrary to everyday experience. Often a phone call or letter, or an email, would be the first step on a fascinating voyage of discovery. One more intriguing incident that, scientists would have us believe, 'simply shouldn't happen'. An event such as an encounter with a ghost that challenges the everyday reality we take for granted. Is the world no more than that which we see around us? Or does Glasgow interact with a range of 'worlds'? Ones that are normally invisible, but can sometimes have a definite effect on our own reality though the reasons why may often be unclear. Is this evidence for the 'parallel universes' that some physicists argue exist? Whatever the explanation *Haunted Glasgow* is full of such strange cases. Cases that offer a challenge to the way in which we view the everyday world.

Is man, for example, alone in the universe? Do UFOs prove that there are other life forms? But what exactly is a UFO? Is it a craft from a distant planet? A glimpse into our future? And are UFOs as harmless as some observers claim? One fact is undeniable. Glasgow has become a hotbed of UFO activity as described by many credible witnesses. The experiences of James Welsh, as recounted in *Haunted Glasgow*, offer an amazing insight into the UFO phenomenon. Whatever your view the evidence is laid out in *Haunted Glasgow* and its dramatic nature is unarguable, whatever conclusion you may come to about the nature of the phenomenon.

Some phenomena are more disturbing than others. The sight of a phantom, even one that moves, will no doubt result in an uneasy night's sleep for most of us. But what if the phantom sets out not only to wreck your home, but also attacks you and at the same time is quite invisible? The poltergeist, recorded throughout history, must surely rank as one of the most bizarre of all entities. Although 'poltergeist' means simply 'noisy spirit', which suggests an almost playful aspect, events in the city, as documented in *Haunted Glasgow*, suggest a far more sinister aspect. In the case of John Adams the phenomena claimed at one time to be the spirits of the dead; at another they claimed to be demons from a different world and behaved in what can only be described as a threatening manner. The fact that the poltergeist in this and other incidents appears to have no clear motive makes the events both worrying and perplexing. Are poltergeists engaged in activity we simply don't understand, but which have a real, though hidden, impact on our world? *Haunted Glasgow* may give the open-minded reader some clues.

Finally, and perhaps most challenging of all, there is the issue of the ultimate crime and its links to the paranormal. Do individuals kill as part of a magic ritual to gain control over beings from other worlds? Or are people driven by entities from other dimensions to commit murder? There is evidence for both scenarios from several horrific incidents that have taken place within the city and I have examined the events in detail. It is hard to believe that murder is more than the actions of a twisted mind, but the possibility that there is more going on than is apparent at first glance needs to be considered. Could 'ritual killing' really be a well-hidden aspect of Glasgow society?

Of course, as many writers have pointed out before, no book is an island and this one also benefits from the thoughts and experiences of past and present writers even where they have written on subjects far removed from the paranormal. There are a range of people, witnesses, investigators and writers, past and present, to whom I am indebted. I'd like to thank Dr Peter McCue for introducing me to James Montgomery and making me aware of the details of these fascinating events. Any interpretation of the incidents I take full responsibility for. I'd also like to thank everyone whose experiences I have documented for giving, in various ways, accounts of their experience. Some have been happy to give their real names; others have requested that their identities be concealed. In a number of instances I have concealed real names. I'm aware that life moves on and cases where people were willing to be publicly identified a decade or more ago, but are now out of contact, they might feel more reluctant today. I do appreciate their willingness to have shared their experience in a public forum. I'd like to thank James Welsh, John Adams, Kenneth, James Montgomery, George Byng, Arlene Russo, Sam Cawley and Gary Gray. A variety of writers and investigators past and present have enlightened me through their publications in the process of writing *Haunted Glasgow*, including Malcolm Robinson, Harry Bell, Carol Foreman, Peter Cowan, Elliott O'Donnell, Catherine Crowe, Ronnie Scott, Stephen Terry, Terence Whittaker, Paul Devereux, Jenny Randles,

Richard Fawcett, Karen Ralls-Macleod, Ian Robertson, Thomas Davidson and Michael Hunter among others and I would certainly recommend their books to the reader. I would also like to thank my wife Evelyn for assisting with research and for her tolerance while I spent so much time working on *Haunted Glasgow*.

Last, but not least, I would like to thank my publishers, Fort Publishing, for their continued interest in the subject of the paranormal and the support that has made this book possible.

**Ron Halliday, Bridge of Allan**
**August 2008**

# 1

# Mystic People

People are at the heart of *Haunted Glasgow*. Individual experience is the channel by which those 'other worldly' events come to public attention. Certain characters, however, have inevitably stamped their mark on the city. They have provided the backdrop and encapsulated in their lives the mystic essence at the heart of the city. If it is asked, 'What is haunted Glasgow?' you need look no further than the events witnessed by a range of individuals and the strange lives of a few. Take the city's founder and inspiration: St Kentigern. He possessed the sort of paranormal powers you'd usually find in a wizard or mystic. He brought a dead bird back to life. He caused fire to break out on a frozen branch. He made the ground rise to form a hill, Dovehill. He could make objects move through time and space. These magical powers and the mystical events associated with this mysterious individual live with us today, emblazoned on Glasgow's coat of arms. A mystic symbol with magical origins about which few of us are aware. There you will see the bird resurrected by St Kentigern. And the tree, a branch of which burst into flames at Kentigern's command. And the hill he raised by magic. And the fish, which is a strange tale in itself.

Kentigern was asked for help in finding a ring which the King of Strathclyde, Rhydderch Heal, had given to his wife. She, how-ever, had been having an affair and had given her lover the ring. The King, meanwhile, heard whispers that his wife was deceiving him and decided on a test to find out the truth. Having got hold of the ring and thrown it into the Clyde, he asked the Queen to give him back the ring as proof that she had not been unfaithful. The Queen knew that her life depended on retrieving it and begged holy man Kentigern for help. Kentigern asked a monk to hook the

first fish that he came across. He followed St Kentigern's instruct-
ions and, inside the salmon, the Queen's ring was discovered.

One can see this account on many levels and not just as a curious fairy story. It has echoes of a Good Samaritan tale, with St
Kentigern helping a woman in distress and a queen to boot. But
there's surely a lot more to it than that. As a ring, a circle, is the
symbol of life and eternity then it's understandable why it might
play a part in this story. It is also a symbol of femininity. A fish
represents Christ, but also the Fisher King, a key player underlying
many of Britain's ancient mythical stories. He was the guardian of
the otherworld, who became in Christian tradition the protector
of the Holy Grail. So this traditional tale of St Kentigern must, in
some way obvious to his compatriots, but less clear to us, represent
aspects of his persona. Given the mythical pagan elements mixed
in, it undoubtedly strengthens the view of St Kentigern as a bridge
between pagan beliefs and the gradual transformation of Scotland
into a Christian society.

Indeed, the circumstances of St Kentigern's birth define him
as an 'other worldly' creature, part of this world, but with links to
a mythical dimension. His mother, Enoch, was the daughter of a
king of Lothian. She fell pregnant but, as she was not married, her
father had her thrown from the top of Traprain Law. She was
miraculously saved, but the King then set his daughter out on a
boat alone on the Firth of Forth. Here she was escorted by a shoal
of fish till she landed safely in Culross on the Fife coast, where St
Kentigern was born. Enoch, later St Enoch, has her own links with
the city and is said to have lived here beside a sacred well. She is
commemorated in the name St Enoch's Square, among others.

There's also an old rhyme connected to the city's coat of arms
which refers to 'the bird that never flew', 'the tree that never grew'
and 'the fish that never swam'. The meaning is obscure, though
there may be some clues. The bird is a thing of the air, the tree that
of the earth and the fish of the water. In the ancient world it was
believed, even by the elite, that all material objects were formed

from a combination of earth, air, water and fire. Stories about St Kentigern involve his ability to control exactly these elements as signified in his resurrection of the robin, setting fire to a branch and the recovery of a gold ring from the fish. Although the city's emblem displays an oak tree the original story told of St Kentigern describes his power over a hazel branch. A hazel would make more sense. It was the most magical plant in the eyes of the pagan Celts and eating its nuts enhanced psychic ability. Curiously, in view of St Kentigern's feat, hazel was seen as a protection against lightning and fire.

There were other strange tales told about Kentigern. There were no men to turn the fields so he ordered two deer to yoke themselves to the plough, which they dutifully did. They carried on working the land till one day a wolf appeared and killed and ate one of the deer. St Kentigern then ordered the wolf to take the stag's place which it did. No doubt there are levels of meaning to this tale, which, of course, isn't meant to be taken literally. It reveals St Kentigern's mystic character as a person who was in tune with, and could control, the forces of nature. A man who could tame the untameable and who makes the hunter and the hunted work together. It's probably not surprising to learn that St Kentigern had a 'magic stick', which would, in all likelihood, have been shaped like a long, curved wand. Experts have judged that it would have been less than three feet in length and might have been made of thorn as was that of St Malloch. And thorn has a long tradition as a mystical tree as its branches are used in a range of magic spells.

St Kentigern, as a religious leader, might have been expected to take a close interest in the 'invisible world'. But in other characters it seems less obvious or even at odds with their public persona. Donald Dewar's links with Glasgow were strong. He was born here, went to Glasgow Academy then Glasgow University and his legal practice was based in the city. He served as MP for Garscadden, winning the seat in a historic victory against the SNP in 1978. After he died a remarkable statue was erected to Scotland's first First Minister in the square outside Buchanan Galleries shopping centre. So why was Donald Dewar so obsessed with siting Scotland's first parliament for three hundred years in Edinburgh? And in one area of Edinburgh in particular? There's little doubt that it was Dewar, more than anyone, who believed in the Holyrood site. Of all the locations in Edinburgh, it was the most mystical. It was here that King David I was saved from being gored to death by a stag, a creature with a lengthy 'otherworld' pedigree, by divine intervention. And the site stands in the shadow of Arthur's Seat with its long-standing 'magical' tradition as the home of fairies, ghosts and, most recently, UFOs. Donald Dewar was well aware of the area's historic roots, praising them in a well-publicised press release. So in spite of an ever-escalating cost and a strange design for the new building by architect Enrico Miralles, Dewar pressed on. It reveals another side to Donald Dewar. A hidden interest in the mystical that so characterises Glasgow's own history. An ability to have a practical attitude to moneymaking – Dewar died a multi-millionaire to the amazement of even his closest acquaintances – that can sit without contradicting an interest in a less worldly view of life. How else can you explain his determination to build the world's most bizarrely shaped parliament building at a site replete with mystical associations?

Mysticism does not spring to mind when the activities of political or military leaders are considered, but it is more common than might be guessed as Tony Blair and Ronald Reagan (both with Scottish bloodlines) show. And, moving to a more heroic age, for too long the mystical side of William Wallace has been overlooked. It might be said that Wallace's stature as a national hero is so great that he belongs to all of Scotland. But Wallace does have an important connection to Glasgow. Although his birthplace is uncertain recent tradition has claimed him for Elderslie, a few miles from the city. Some have even argued he was born in Glasgow itself and that at least in later years he had strong associations with the city. The truth is that much is obscure about Wallace's life. Even the year of his birth is a mystery. But one fact in all the myth is clear: it was in Glasgow that Wallace was hiding in 1305 when he was captured and handed over to Edward. Is it too much to speculate that Wallace had returned to Scotland's spiritual centre for guidance? There is a basis to suggest this could be the case. For centuries historians have ignored the mystical Wallace because it does not fit in with our 'Braveheart' image of Scotland's greatest, and certainly most popular, hero. But there is no doubt that there was a less worldly side to Wallace. He was, in fact, in contact with, and took advice from, entities from other worlds. This is not as strange as it appears. Tony and Cherie Blair consulted a spiritual guru, Elizabeth I of England had her white magician, John Dee, and Ronald Reagan took advice from an astrologer. One of the earliest accounts of Wallace's life describes how he visited Monkton kirk in Ayrshire and went into a deep sleep or trance. In this shaman-like state Wallace had a vision. He saw a brilliant ball of fire coming down from the sky. It moved towards him and then landed beside him. Out of the fire a woman appeared, surrounded by a dazzling light. She handed Wallace a wand, coloured red and green, and, with a sapphire, made a sign across his face, usually interpreted as the Saltire. The other worldly significance of the colours green and blue are obvious. Red represents rebirth, as in the phoenix rising from the ashes. The mysterious figure then spoke to Wallace, gave him a book and disappeared in a ball of light back to the sky. Wallace then emerged from his trance.

Change the century and it sounds similar to encounters claimed by alien contactees today. Or, perhaps, more correctly, a meeting with some angel-like figure. Wallace, being Wallace, did not, of course, interpret it that way. He saw it as a sign to carry on the struggle for independence, and the rest is history. However, it reveals a different side of the man and, perhaps, explains why he was gradually sidelined. A person in receipt of messages from other worlds must have seemed on a divine mission, which probably didn't go down well with the hard-headed cynics running Scotland at the time. It's not surprising that the Earl of Buchan, an eccentric mystic, who dabbled in the occult and built a Greek temple on his lands in the Borders, erected an enormous statue of Wallace overlooking this ancient replica. He, almost alone, recognised the mystical side to Scotland's greatest hero.

The idea of alien beings or entities from other dimensions influencing our day-to-day existence seems hard to credit, yet according to some, such incidents happen on a regular basis. Not, obviously, with the dramatic effect occasioned by Wallace's experience, but these entities can guide and lead us down different paths. It can even lead to mass suicide. When St Kentigern lay dying he claimed, as described in Bishop Jocelyn's *Wife of Kentigern*, that he was being visited by an entity which he described as an angel. The entity, angel or not, in fact encouraged Kentigern to commit suicide. The being told the saint to arrange for 'a warm bath to be prepared', which would let him 'pass away without pain'. However, not only was the 'angel' willing to help St Kentigern to carry out suicide, but the entity also encouraged his followers to die with him. He was told by this being from another world that if anyone else stepped into the bath 'before the water cooled' they would 'pass quietly away'. The event was scheduled for the Christian feast of the Epiphany, which is traditionally celebrated on 6 January, but the description of the event makes it seem like a strange magic rite. Or a contemporary science-fiction plot where a vortex is opened to another world. Certainly an event far removed from our present-day image of Christian practice. As the sun rose 'the holy man . . . entered a vessel of hot water, which he had first blessed with the sign of salvation'. Around the bath stood a circle of his followers waiting for their leader to die. St Kentigern had been in the water for only a short time when he raised his hands skywards then lowered his head 'as if in a deep sleep'. Kentigern was dead. Then followed mass suicide. His disciples took the saint's body out of the bath and 'eagerly strove with each other to enter the water and so, one by one, before the water cooled' they all died with their leader. St Kentigern was unquestionably an outstanding individual, but even outstanding men can be duped. What was this entity that so influenced him? Why was it so keen to persuade others to die? It's interesting that St Kentigern met with St Columba in Glasgow. Columba was another who regularly communicated with entities from other worlds on a hill on the island of Iona. Iona, like Glasgow, had strong links to Druidism as the island was one of the last strongholds of that pagan religion.

Especially intriguing are the links between St Kentigern and Merlin. There is no doubt that King Arthur – whether of myth, legend or fact – has strong links with Scotland. And that is even truer of his shaman – the wizard or priest, Merlin. Spelt 'Myrddin', a stained-glass window in Stobbo church in the Scottish Borders shows Merlin kneeling in front of St Kentigern. Merlin may be shown in an inferior position, allegedly converting to Christianity, but the implication is clear. Kentigern and the pagan Merlin share a common bond. Merlin was said to have lived wild among the woods of the Borders, where he had fled after the death of Arthur following the battle of Arthuret. Merlin had a special link with nature: he could talk to wolves and birds, which chimes with St Kentigern's relationship with these creatures. The window in Stobbo church does not date from the time of St Kentigern, but it confirms an ancient tradition of a connection between Merlin and Kentigern. And Kentigern would have lived around the time Arthur and Merlin were alive. But that is by no means the only link between Glasgow and the Arthurian era.

It has been claimed that an ancient coffin carved out of a single, solid stone, discovered in Govan Old parish church in 1885, contained the body of King Arthur. This is on the grounds that the stone is marked with an 'A' and has not been engraved with any Christian symbols. It also seems to be decorated with a Celtic-style warrior. Although it is not possible to prove that this is Arthur's resting place it does demonstrate the long-standing tradition of a link between Arthur and Glasgow. Not forgetting that at nearby

Dumbarton Rock we have Arthur's Seat and the site itself has been linked to the very Rhydderch Hael whose wife, by tradition, St Kentigern allegedly saved. She was also, by tradition, Merlin's sister Gwynedd. It's certainly true that many areas have claimed Arthur as their own, including north and south Wales, the Scottish Borders and Cornwall. However, Scotland, in the land between the Borders and Glasgow, has a strong tradition of both Arthur's and Merlin's presence. This is based on a genuine folk memory and suggests that at the very least they may have been active in the area at one time. Of course, separating fact and fiction from a past so distant that few records have survived is notoriously difficult. It is even argued that neither Arthur nor Merlin existed so it may be that the traditions surrounding them reflect a set of values and beliefs. This would fit with the 'history' that has developed round St Kentigern. The accounts of his life are a mass of contradictions, but what all the tales do is confirm a character who was part mystic and seems to have absorbed much of the 'magic' that attached itself to religious leaders of a pre-Christian outlook. And this could explain why St Kentigern is linked with Merlin, as a bridge between different eras.

Given the scant written records, it's difficult to pin down the course of events. We can get only the occasional glimpse into the swirling current of history. Beyond Merlin, Arthur and St Kentigern are those anonymous people never to be known. The men and women who have come down to us only as Druids or pagans. These were the builders of stone circles, the inhabitants of the sacred ground which the necropolis and cathedral now occupy and of other mystic sites long gone. We may not know their names, but we can certainly respect their contribution to the city. They were the first to recognise and appreciate the mystic aura of this area. But when we skip forward to more recent times, where individuals are more readily identifiable and we have more evidence to mull over, we can see that though the people may change the mystical theme carries on even when not immediately obvious.

Only recently has the mystical side of Charles Rennie Mackintosh and his wife Margaret been recognised. Mackintosh was not famous in his lifetime. Indeed he would probably have been astonished to learn that he would become to future generations the icon he is today. He was born in June 1868 in Parson Street, but when he was six moved to Firpark Terrace in Dennistoun. In view of the mystical nature of his work it was a fitting address, situated so close to the Cathedral and the hill of the Necropolis. During his lifetime and for decades thereafter the mystical symbolism in Mackintosh's work was no more than hinted at and largely ignored as an aberration. It's only recently that it has begun to dawn that Mackintosh, along with his wife Margaret, were more than brilliant designers of furniture and buildings. They inscribed within their work a range of meanings, which we are only now beginning to decipher. Of course, not everything that Mackintosh and his wife were involved with was necessarily symbolic, but within many designs deeper meanings were hidden. An obvious example is a painting by Margaret Mackintosh of a baby in a rose. A rose is a symbolic womb and when the broader work of Charles and Margaret is examined the rose symbol appears time and time again. A rose, to initiates, can have many levels of meaning which is why it is an emblem adopted by many secret societies. It can represent life, rebirth and a link with the 'other world'. A rose, of course, is also a sign representing femininity. In Hill House you can experience the effort expanded by Charles and Margaret to balance male and female elements. The Yin and Yang of life, which together make for a more balanced and fulfilling existence. In Hill House Charles made prolific use of squares, which appear everywhere on furniture, decoration and even the shape of the windows. And a square in mystical geometric symbolism stands for a man and masculinity. A circle by contrast represents woman and femininity. Colours were also used throughout the couple's work to balance masculine and feminine elements, which again is very much in evidence at Hill House. Purple and blue for the male, pink and white for the female. In the dining room at Hill House the significance of wall decorations have been disputed. Are they of a vase, or, as some experts have suggested, the stylised naked body of Mackintosh's wife Margaret? And take a plaster panel called 'the willow tree'. In reality it looks as remote from a tree as one can imagine and even authorities on Mackintosh accept that it looks more like a man. I would suggest that it looks not only like a man, but also is in the image of some ancient Egyptian god, man-god or priest standing before the gates of a temple. The fact that this strange picture was labelled 'willow tree' suggests that Mackintosh was taking a deliberate decision to hide deeper meanings in his work. There were certainly stylised versions of the Tree of Life within Mackintosh's work. It's a symbol that predates Christianity, the best-known example being the giant ash tree of Viking mythology, known as Yggdrasil, which, according to their religion, held up the sky and connected the world of the living to the underworld ruled by the dead. It's a symbol of the ancient belief that life, death and rebirth are all part of one mystical process.

For a house decoration in Derngate Mackintosh produced what is in essence overlapping pyramid shapes with, replicating the design of the Great Pyramid at Giza, an overlapping sheath of white. This has long been stripped from the ancient pyramids, but originally they were covered in a layer of marble to make these huge structures glisten in the sun. In the Mackintosh dining room, reconstructed in the Hunterian art gallery, there sits a typical long-backed Mackintosh table-chair, except that the head rest is shaped like an enormous eye with a round hole where the pupil would be. Clearly, this is reminiscent of the all-seeing eye of ancient Egypt, sometimes mistakenly referred to as the 'evil eye'. Another example was displayed at a Mackintosh memorial exhibition in 1933.

In fact, everywhere you look in Mackintosh's work symbolism leaps out. How influential Mackintosh's wife Margaret was on his work is much debated, but the sexual mysticism within her *Heart of the Rose* panel is plain to see. Mackintosh certainly seems to have bonded together the mystical tradition of the West with an admiration for the religious mysteries of the East. However, there is much about his and his wife's work which remains unexplained.

The architect Alexander Thomson predated Mackintosh. His obsession was with Egypt, though he is better known as 'Greek' Thomson because of his designs based on the style of the ancient Greeks. It's not clear whether Thomson or Mackintosh had their own mystical experiences. Some individuals seem to bring mysticism to their work and are imbued with its spirit. Others experience it and we can all learn from such events.

An amazing number of Glaswegians have contacted me over the years about experiences they have been through outside the city. Is this the Glasgow phenomenon – to have more attuned psychic senses? The experience of Partick resident David McArthur is representative of many. He told me:

> I was driving along the A823. It wasn't especially late, but it was dark and I was tired as I'd been on the go all day. I switched on the radio to try and keep myself awake. But it was a struggle. And then on a deserted stretch of road it just happened. I saw something shining in the road ahead of me. I slowed down and as I got closer I saw that it was like a glowing human being. Except it had huge wings on its back. It just looked at me and then smiled. Then vanished. The strangest thing is that I thought it looked like my grandfather, who had died when I was young. I don't know if it was a warning, but it kept me wide awake all the way home.

Indeed, Glasgow's citizens have encountered almost every phenomenon that could be imagined, including, in the 1930s, Britain's earliest UFO sighting.

And age is no barrier. Cameron Macaulay believed that he had lived a past life in Barra. What was extraordinary about this was that Cameron was only six at the time, in September 2006. The fact that such a young person could remember what seemed to be the events of a past life hit the headlines across Scotland. Cameron liked drawing pictures of his home for his mum. A single storey, white-painted building that overlooked a bay. But what was truly bizarre was that Cameron lived in Clydebank. The house he drew, the building he called home, was nearly two hundred miles away in a place he'd never seen. It turned out that Cameron had talked a lot over the years about his life on the island of Barra. He could remember his father dying and said his name was Shane Robertson. He described having brothers and sisters as well. To Cameron, though only six years old, his life on Barra was a very powerful memory. In fact, he became upset at times thinking of his family there and how they would be missing him. Even at nursery he cried because he missed Barra so much and especially playing with his brothers and sisters. He wanted to let them know that he was fine. As part of a television documentary, broadcast on Channel 5, Cameron was taken to Barra. In his Clydebank home, he had talked about seeing planes landing on a beach from his house, and, on Barra, this is where the landing strip is located. Investigation unearthed a white house beside a bay, which had once been owned by a family called Robertson. There was, however, no one called Shane. The Robertson family had, it was said, owned a black car and a dog, just as Cameron claimed. Even stranger was the fact that the white house had three toilets, just as Cameron described. It all seemed a good bit more than coincidence. However, the strangest part is the way in which Cameron told of how he had arrived in Clydebank with Norma as his mum. He explained that he had fallen through and 'gone into' Norma's tummy. On the face of it, it sounded like a case suggestive of reincarnation. Adults I have talked to, who believe they have lived a 'past life', have described to me the experience of being asked, after they die, what kind of life they wish to be reincarnated in. And making a choice. Cameron's experience seems more haphazard than that. 'Falling through' something suggests almost an accident like walking into a time anomaly. It's a very strange case. Cameron seemed convinced by the reality of a previous life in Barra and his experience is reflected by accounts from elsewhere in the world involving young children. The most famous would surely be that of successive Tibetan Dalai Lamas, who are believed to be reincarnated in a young child. When their religious leader dies, Tibetan Buddhists make a search for the boy who has received his spirit and who will be the next Dalai Lama.

For hundreds of years religion has been an integral part of Glasgow city life. But even so no one could have expected that events in Glasgow would lead to the canonisation of the first Scottish saint for seven hundred years. In March 1967 former dock worker John Fagan lay seriously ill in his home in Penston Road on the Queenslie estate. John, originally from Anderston, was a modest man who had, in his twenties, served with the Royal Scots in Italy during the second world war. After being demobbed John returned to Glasgow and settled back to working in the Clyde dockyards. He was a man who got on with life, rarely complaining, and with his wife Mary raised six children. In fact, John was such a quiet character that he took a while to mention the stomach pains, which, by spring 1965, when he was in his early fifties, were dulling his appetite and causing him considerable discomfort. It was his wife Mary who eventually persuaded John to see a doctor. But what was first thought to be a stomach ulcer was diagnosed as cancer after John was examined by specialists. Immediate action was called for. Surgeons operated in May 1965, but though the growth in his stomach was safely removed secondary tumours developed. It was devastating news and John was given only months to live. But John Fagan in his quiet, but determined, way clung on to life, even though his weight had dropped from eleven to five stones and he was by the early months of 1967 unable to move from his bed. By then the hospital experts had given up on John Fagan and sent him home to die with his family at his bedside to offer him some comfort. And by the early hours of Monday, 6 March John's situation appeared critical. He seemed to have only minutes left as life ebbed rapidly away. John muttered a few words, which might have been 'I'm going', but it was only a statement that was obvious to everyone around. He was skin and bone and it was hardly possible to detect even a heartbeat.

So who or what intervened so dramatically to change John's condition? It was as if some invisible angel had waved a magic wand. One moment death's door beckoned, but then, incredibly, John seemed to recover in an instant. He spoke to his wife Mary, who was at his bedside, telling her that he was hungry, he hadn't eaten for weeks and that he felt 'so different'. His remarkable recovery astonished doctors who moved him from his 'death bed' back to hospital, an immediate recognition of the transformation that had taken place in John's health. An investigation of the tumours which had been destroying John's body found that they had simply disappeared. So what had led to such a miraculous improvement? A medallion had been pinned to John's pyjamas as he lay ill. It depicted John Ogilvie, a Catholic priest, who had been hanged at Glasgow Cross in 1615. A man who had lived a short, but eventful, life. Ogilvie was born in 1580, the son of an affluent family near the town of Keith in Banffshire. His father, Walter Ogilvie, brought John up in the Calvinist tradition, but, while being educated in Europe as a teenager, John converted to Catholicism. In 1610 he was ordained as a Jesuit priest in Paris. Although he had been out of his native land for many years he was determined to return and by 1613 he was secretly ministering to Catholics across central Scotland. But within a year he was betrayed and arrested in Glasgow. Held in jail Ogilvie was tortured in an effort to force him to reveal the names of those families who had welcomed him into their homes. His legs were crushed by chaining metal bars around his shins, then battering them with hammers. At other times red-hot needles were forced into his chest and body. The pain must have been excruciating. Showing incredible strength of will Ogilvie defied his torturers and refused to divulge any information about his Catholic flock. Put on trial at the Bishop's castle – which once stood beside Glasgow cathedral but has long since been demolished – Ogilvie was charged and convicted of high treason. He was executed, at Glasgow Cross, immediately after the declaration of the verdict, on 10 March 1615. However, the manner in which he had endured the torture, and his calm acceptance of death, won him many admirers. People soon began praying for the departed soul of John Ogilvie and believed they were getting a response. Through the following centuries many were convinced that they had been cured of illness thanks to his intervention. But before John Fagan's near-death recovery none had been classified as miraculous. However, the evidence this time, for believers, seemed all too clear. In addition to the medal that well-wishers had pinned to John's pyjamas, prayers had been offered up to Ogilvie in an attempt to persuade his 'spirit' to intervene. And every night John's wife Mary had quietly asked John Ogilvie for help in saving her husband. So had these prayers brought about divine intercession?

However you look at it, Fagan's recovery was surely a miracle. He was permanently cured of an illness that had brought him seconds from death and by the spring of 1968 was back at work in the docks. He lived for another twenty-five years till he passed away in the town of Livingston in 1993 at the age of seventy-nine. But how did John himself describe that instant moment of magic when he made such a dramatic recovery? In fact, what he remembered is similar to many near-death experiences across the globe. He recounted feeling, as he lay dying, that he was looking at the gates of heaven. Then he saw his long-dead auntie, Annie. She was 'dressed in her Sunday best' and seemed to be signalling to him to come through the gates. Then the vision faded and John woke up feeling hungry. The 'miracle' of John Fagan's recovery attracted worldwide attention and there was soon a campaign to have John Ogilvie's role in that recovery recognised. A panel of medical experts, of all faiths, was set up to investigate John's illness and his nature-defying recovery. After examining all the evidence from hospital files the panel's verdict rocked the world of science. It concluded, after several years' work, that there was no natural explanation for the sudden disappearance of John's tumours and the instant improvement in his health. It was an amazing turn of events for a man who had worked his whole life quietly in the dockyards of Glasgow and described his religious beliefs before the dramatic days of 1967 as no more than 'wishy-washy'. Because of his experience, he told people almost in disbelief, John Ogilvie, the man family and friends had prayed to, was about to be raised to the sainthood. On 17 October 1976, in an event that attracted huge global publicity, several thousand Scots, including Cardinal Gray and Archbishop Winning, travelled to Rome to witness the canonisation of John Ogilvie by Pope Paul VI. They were among a crowd of some twenty thousand packed into St Peter's. Also present were Princess Alexandra with her husband Angus Ogilvy, a descendant, it is said, of John Ogilvie's family. During the service a new bagpipe march, composed by John MacDonald of the Glasgow Police pipe band, and dedicated to St John Ogilvie, was played to set the seal on a truly Scottish event, but one that had stirred the whole world. John Ogilvie was Scotland's first saint since Queen Margaret was raised to the sainthood in 1250 and is the only post-Reformation Scot to be honoured in this way. And all because of a quietly spoken Glasgow dockyard worker. The events that took place in 1967 at John Fagan's modest council house in working class Queenslie are surely proof that miracles not only can, but do, happen.

John Fagan didn't have any warning that illness was going to devastate his life, so why should some people have premonitions and not others? In 1999 Cora Buchanan from Elderslie was lucky to escape injury when a chimney stack crashed through the ceiling and flattened the bed on which, just moments before, she had been lying. The twelve-year-old, hearing a creaking sound, remembered the dream that her mum, Diana, had told her about three weeks before. In it her mum was warned that something bad was going to happen to Cora. She had told her daughter of this and so when Cora heard an unusual noise overhead the link flashed through her mind and she rushed to get out of her bedroom. Just in time as it turned out. But events of this nature leave many unanswered questions. Why did Diana have the dream and not Cora? And why was she given a warning when others aren't so lucky? It's almost as if, by chance, a phone line to the future opened up and Diana, luckily for Cora, was plugged into it.

Some aspects of the city, however, seem to defy explanation. The Tontine faces, which once adorned the town hall, were a source of much dispute. What were they and who were they intended to represent? In all, there were ten sculpted heads, but the weird expressions that had been carved on the faces meant that they appeared distinctly non-human not to say positively weird. It was believed they dated from the 1740s when the town hall was erected at Glasgow Cross and their sculptors, it was argued, must be either Mungo Naismith or David Cation. Whoever was responsible, however, must have had a real interest in the city's distant pagan roots. For with our reawakened awareness of pagan symbolism there is no doubt that several of the faces have been carved to represent the 'green man', the ruler of nature. From the heads of several sprout broad leaves and other foliage. One has a necklace of shells. Representations that can also be found in Glasgow cathedral and Rosslyn chapel. But it's odd to find the pagan god on a building with no obvious religious connection. It may be, though, that the figures had significance for some of the council members. Part, maybe, of the mystic network that seems to have been active behind the outward face of the city at various times in its history. It's a fascinating glimpse of the hidden forces at work in the past.

But in the last few decades the psychic side of Glasgow has once more come to the fore. I have been in touch with many of the city's psychics in recent years and gained many fascinating insights. In the late 1990s I interviewed psychic medium Gary Gray for my

'X-Files' column in the *Evening Times*[1]. Like many gifted mediums he seems to have had the ability to see into other worlds from an early age. He told me that he was only nine when he encountered his first spirit. During the night he got up to visit the toilet and when he opened his bedroom door a silver-haired man, whom Gary didn't recognise, was standing outside. Gary received a bigger shock when the man simply faded away. When he told his parents of his encounter they took out their old photographs to show him snaps of long-dead relatives. Gary quickly pointed to one and said: 'That's him'. The picture was that of an uncle of his mother, an insurance man, who had been murdered on Glasgow Green in the 1920s.

But even before this incident, at a time that he was too young to remember, Gary Gray related how his parents couldn't avoid noticing certain things, as he explained: 'They would hear voices in my room as if I was talking, but there would be no one there. Objects would move by themselves when I was near them. When I was four I caught my arm in an electric wringer. It was being pulled in and would have been pulped. Incredibly, the mangle just switched off.'

By the time I met Gary in 1998 he had a 'spirit guide', a helper from the other side. A spirit guide comes through from the world beyond to assist a medium to develop their natural psychic abilities. Gary's guide had been a down-and-out, who had walked the streets of Glasgow in the 1930s. However, a medium may have more than one spirit helper and Gary has at least two others who help him. One is a wee lad called George. According to Gary: 'Every night I feel the presence of George. He's a young boy. The first time he came I was feeling down over the death of my dad. I felt this little hand patting my back as if to say "you're not on your own".' More recently Gary's twin, Stephen, who died in 2007, has been working from the spirit world with Gary. But perhaps his most amazing experience was to encounter the spirit of his father, who died some months before we met. Gary recalled, 'It happened when I had an out-of-body experience. I saw a wall of bricks light up like the gable end of a house. And then I was there – wherever it is you go. I saw my dad and he said, "Gary, there is life. Everyone experiences it. You have to go on".'

Gary's glimpses of the spirit world have given him a vivid impression of what life after death is like. 'I have seen the spirit world and it's much like this one without the same aggression. I've seen a place called the Hall of Learning. It's like a massive library. People are just like they are here, but with their rugged edges smoothed.' It's a fascinating insight denied to most of us. Gary described his psychic abilities as 'a gift', which is a sentiment echoed by many with the ability to communicate with other worlds. The experience of people who can 'lift the veil' to other worlds is startling evidence that, at the very least, the world does not fit into a neat category. Even as the twenty-first century rolled in the city's fascination with the 'other world' continued unabated. One of the most popular features in the *Evening Times* was the 'Ruth the Truth' column, in which psychic Ruth Urquhart responded to readers' queries on a range of issues both emotional and practical. Meanwhile, for those interested in vampires, Britain's only magazine devoted to the subject, *Bite Me*, edited by Arlene Russo, started life in 1999 and continues to be published in Glasgow. Even the Indian mystic Sai Baba had a lodge of followers in the city.

Glasgow's most recent internationally known psychic is medium Gordon Smith. At one time known as the 'psychic barber', Smith has won worldwide renown with his ability to convey messages from the spirits of the dead and has a long list of endorsements from famous people. What makes Gordon Smith stand out, witnesses explain, is his ability to pass on detailed information. He has recounted his experiences in a series of books, books that provide remarkable evidence that it is possible to communicate with spirit entities. There might well be disagreement on exactly who these entities are, and what they represent, but the evidence for there being *something* beyond our own world is very strong. There is no doubt that 'mystical Glasgow' will carry on, whatever the gritty image the city presents to the world. There is a deeper side that will surely inspire the spiritual awareness of future generations.

## Note

[1] Ron Halliday, 'That's The Spirit', *Evening Times*, 14 November 1998

# 2

# Mystic Sites

When we think of Scotland's mystic sites it has to be admitted that Glasgow does not spring immediately to mind. Thoughts turn instead to the nation's ancient capital, Edinburgh, and it seems to have been forgotten that Glasgow, unlike Edinburgh, was actually founded as a religious centre. It was here, fifteen hundred years ago, that the Christian mystic, Kentigern, later to be raised to sainthood, set up a church as a base from which to convert Scotland from its pagan roots. Kentigern chose this spot because it already possessed an ancient mystic tradition and was a gathering point for Druids, who had their sanctuary on Fir Park where the necropolis, Glasgow's famous city of the dead, now stands. The Druids had been attracted to this area because of some undefined magical quality they instinctively recognised. My own investigation has revealed that there was something special in this landscape, specifically the area that surrounds the present cathedral, which mystics believed facilitated contact with other worlds. The evidence reveals a complex thread that links the centre of the city to a weird mixture of supernatural events, goblins, underground tunnels and the mysterious force known as ley lines. Over the centuries the mystical origins of the city have gradually been forgotten, buried, not only literally, but also psychologically, beneath centuries of urban sprawl. So much so that it may come as a shock when the question is put: is Glasgow the true resting place of the Holy Grail? The Grail is the sacred vessel said to have been used by Jesus Christ at the Last Supper and later acquired by Joseph of Arimathea, who reputedly filled it with Christ's blood after he was crucified. For many it has miraculous powers.

Many sites have been put forward as the location for the Grail, most recently Rosslyn chapel near Edinburgh. But can Glasgow really have the stronger claim? In fact, Glasgow cathedral could be the missing piece of a jigsaw that links the Grail, Rosslyn chapel and other key mystic sites. Is it possible that Glasgow cathedral, by far the older of the two buildings, was the original resting place either of the Grail or of other important artefacts linked to Jesus? Objects that were at some time transferred to Rosslyn? Or was Rosslyn built as a secret sign to where the Grail was truly believed to lie? In Glasgow. To some the Grail is not an object but an idea. Could the idea have been a secret pact between early Christians and pagans? To fuse the two religions into one? This would explain much of the pagan symbolism that so surprises visitors to important religious sites even today. There are some unexpected links between Rosslyn chapel and Glasgow. Rosslyn chapel is an exact replica of the east choir of Glasgow cathedral. In fact, there is little doubt that when Rosslyn chapel was built it was deliberately designed to be a copy of that particular part of Glasgow's ancient edifice. Glasgow cathedral, like Rosslyn chapel, is covered in carvings that indicate the influence of Freemasons and the Knights Templar. Beneath the stunning visible structure of the cathedral, however, lies an enigmatic building known as the lower church. As a church within a church it is an arrangement unique among Christian sites which, it has been proposed, is an exact replica of Solomon's temple, the site in the Holy Land where it is alleged the Knights Templar discovered the Grail and other sacred objects. It is surely not without significance that Rosslyn chapel too is said to have been constructed in imitation of the ancient temple of Solomon.

Glasgow's founding father, Kentigern (also known as Mungo), provides a further link between Glasgow and Rosslyn. Kentigern was active around Rosslyn and there is a well in the nearby town of Penicuik dedicated to him. It is significant that Kentigern's area of activity also included what would later become a key Knights Templar location at Temple in the Lothians. The mysterious Knights Templar – the reputed discoverers and guardians of the Holy Grail

– were connected with both sites, though, in fact, more closely with Glasgow, thus buttressing the evidence of a mystic link between the two.

So what conclusion can we draw from this? Rosslyn chapel is seen as a place of mystic significance that attracts worldwide attention, yet its design is based on that of Glasgow cathedral. And since William Sinclair, who founded Rosslyn, and those who followed him must have been aware of this fact, it goes without saying that it must have been a deliberate act. This is given added weight by the fact that there is an important family connection between Glasgow cathedral and Rosslyn chapel. Archibald, fifth Earl of Douglas, whose coat of arms, depicting a heart, is carved in the cathedral, was the brother of Margaret Douglas and she was the first wife of William Sinclair, Rosslyn's founder. Archibald was closely involved in the development of the cathedral, giving it financial support. It may well be that Sinclair was encouraged to copy the cathedral's design through learning, from Archibald or Margaret, of its precious secrets. Incidentally, the insignia of the Douglas family, a heart, also appears in Rosslyn chapel, further emphasising the link between the two sites. And, significantly, the Grail and the heart are often connected because of the idea of the sacred blood. The Grail, among other things, was believed to be the object used to gather Christ's holy blood following his crucifixion. All of which suggests that Glasgow's cathedral was seen as a place of great mystic significance. It occupies the exact spot where the city was originally founded, the site chosen by the enigmatic figure of Kentigern, who was following in the footsteps of generations of mystics before him. All of whom had instinctively recognised something 'other worldly' about this spot.

It was Kentigern who gave Glasgow its name. It is generally agreed that the meaning of Glasgow is 'green hollow', a phrase with its own mystic significance. Green was, and still is, the traditional colour of the 'other world', that of the phantom 'green ladies' of ghostly legend, the Green Man of the forest and of fairies and similar creatures. It suggests that Kentigern was well aware of the mystical power generated by the area. So there were good reasons for choosing this site, a hollow overlooked by a hill, on a steep-sided slope, beside a river, to set up his church. For pagans a hollow acted as a portal into another dimension. It linked the everyday world above ground to the underworld inhabited by the spirits of the dead and a host of unearthly creatures. It seems that it was a deliberate decision on Kentigern's part to take over an existing Druidic site, which already possessed a powerful mystical tradition. The ground that includes the cathedral had been regarded as a mystic site for centuries before Kentigern transformed it into a Christian shrine. From across Europe this area had attracted those who wished to commune with other worlds and who believed this stretch of land with its strange forces would help them achieve their goal.

In 2005 writer William Oxenham suggested that the word 'Glasgow' might be of Welsh origin: that is, *glas cae*, the blue field. This, on the surface, might seem to go against an accepted definition of Glasgow as the 'green hollow', but, in fact, it simply adds a bizarre twist. In Scotland, blue, as much as green, was the colour of the 'other world'. So we have the Blue Men of the Minch, mystical creatures of the sea, and the 'blue stone' of St Andrews, by tradition a magic object thrown to earth by the Devil. So is there some strange double meaning attached to the name 'Glasgow', one that not only means the 'green hollow' where the cathedral now stands, but also the mystic area that surrounded it, the 'blue fields' where unearthly creatures roamed and pathways to other worlds opened? The evidence suggests that our ancestors certainly visualised the area in this way. My own research reveals that much of the central area surrounding present-day George Square, now covered by modern buildings, was once an ancient sacred site, which could aptly be labelled the 'blue fields' with the hollow where the cathedral now stands and the hill occupied by the necropolis site as the focus. There existed a mystic heartland, both above and below ground, stretching from the necropolis-cathedral site through

Cowcaddens to Garnethill and down to the raised ground known as Dovehill beside the current Gallowgate.

No one knows for certain exactly when a church was first erected on the 'green hollow'. The cathedral dates to a later period, but it included the remains of earlier structures. But whatever building has stood here might be regarded as secondary, as it is the site itself that resonates with an ancient mystical sanctity. King Edward I of England considered Glasgow cathedral as a place of such mystical significance that he visited it three times. The papacy recognised its 'other worldly' aura by raising it to the status of a special daughter of the Roman Church. It was a site viewed as mystical for hundreds of years before Rosslyn appeared on the scene. To walk into the cathedral and its precincts is to become part of a mystery that stretches back to a pagan past, part of which has been passed down to us through the early Christian saints and was built into the very fabric of the cathedral.

There are many strange aspects to the cathedral. The lower church is a unique building housing the tomb of Kentigern, but that's just the start. The first inkling that there was more to its construction than met the eye did not emerge until early in the nineteenth century. The writer E. C. Morgan – a recognised expert on medieval architecture and Masonic lore – suggested that the architect of the lower church had been attempting to reproduce the layout of the mystical temple of Solomon, the same claim made years later for the design of Rosslyn chapel. It is also significant that, according to Morgan, in the lower church and choir area, there are undeniable signs that the designer was familiar with Masonic symbolism and made use of this knowledge to convey a secret message, one that is not easy to unravel. Again, exactly the same claims have been made in respect of Rosslyn chapel.

It may well be asked why figures of the pagan Green Man, representing the spirits of nature, should be carved in an important Christian building? They can be found in several areas of the cathedral, including the upper choir and lower chapel. Remarkable enough, but perhaps the least of the mysteries. For upon examining the Blacader aisle, built by Archbishop Robert Blacader (1483–1508), the detached observer might wonder just what Christian symbolism the faithful were meant to interpret. You can discover here some truly strange carvings. There is the pure-white skull surrounded by foliage. The bright-red face of the Devil, with an expression somewhere between a leer and a scowl. Dragons and serpents intertwined, echoed in the famous apprentice pillar at Rosslyn, interspersed with pairs of doves, the latter used as a symbol for various emotions and ideas, but closely connected with the Druids and early Christian saints. Is there a secret meaning here? Both the dragon and serpent are highly symbolic. The dragon has often been interpreted as symbolising an energy force used to contact other dimensions by the Druids long before the arrival of Christianity. This link receives further emphasis from a carved band round the doorway of the chapter house in the lower chapel, which, although much worn, appears to show pairs of entwined dragons.

It's as if the architect of Rosslyn looked at Glasgow and decided to copy its pagan, Masonic and Templar symbolism. Unlike Rosslyn chapel, however, the mysterious Knights Templar were directly connected with Glasgow and the cathedral. It is also clear that the Knights Templar had a close interest in Glasgow. We know that as early as 1180 a charter was issued for a plot of land that had been given to the Templars by Jocelyn, Bishop of Glasgow. The charter was issued by Raan Corbeht, master of the temple. The existence of the charter confirms that the bishop of the cathedral had close ties with the Templars. It is significant that the charter dates from the earliest days of the organisation, which was founded in 1119. It is also significant that the Templars were believed to be the guardians of the Holy Grail. Their proper title is the Poor Knights of the Temple of Solomon, in recognition of their connection with Solomon's temple in Jerusalem. This link with the Knights Templar may explain why the design of the Jerusalem temple is believed to be incorporated within Glasgow cathedral and, in turn, within Rosslyn chapel.

But, to appreciate the full mystery of this site, we have to look beyond the immediate area of the cathedral to the surrounding landscape, the mysterious 'blue fields'. Amazing evidence, long hidden, that the central area of Glasgow was at one time a site with a mystical aura can be seen in the names that are linked to the area and have lingered on through the centuries. Take Cowcaddens. Its name originally meant the home of goblins or spirits, weird entities from 'other worlds'. The area known as the Ramshorn also had a tradition of mystery. There is a strange tale told about it that is linked to St Kentigern. A thief seized a ram from his flock and cut off its head, which instantly petrified and stuck to his hands. It proved impossible to remove. Only after he admitted his guilt to Kentigern was he set free; the holy man absolved him and made him a gift of the ram. The scene of this event was afterwards known as the Lands of Ramshorn. An alternative version is that, at rutting time, flocks were brought from the hills to mate with the rams. One night demons provoked the rams and they started fighting each other. In the morning the area was awash with the broken horns of rams, hence 'Ramshorn'. Whatever the explanation it all suggests some bizarre supernatural phenomenon associated with the area, part of a mystical pattern that may explain why the term 'horn', in ancient usage, also denotes a sacred site or enclosure.

And there is more evidence. The Drygate in the city centre is believed to be the oldest surviving thoroughfare in Glasgow. In ancient times – when the Druids worshipped on the sacred groves of Fir Park, now the site of the necropolis – the ritual path to the hill followed the route taken by the Drygate. The word 'dry' is pagan and means priest. It was used to describe the pathway long before the arrival of Christianity. Drygate therefore means the priest's way or road. Was this also the route followed by St Kentigern in a bizarre funeral procession, one that has puzzled successive generations? Jocelyn, a twelfth century Bishop of Glasgow, in his *Life of Kentigern*, described St Kentigern's admiration for 'Fergus', a mysterious figure who appears to have possessed supernatural powers, but of whom little is known. When Fergus died in the sacred oak grove he inhabited near Stirling, Kentigern yoked two untamed bulls to Fergus's funeral cart and took the body from St Ninian's near Stirling 'by a straight road along which there was no path as far as Cathures which is now called Glasgow'. Kentigern then buried Fergus in a cemetery in Glasgow, consecrated by St Ninian, in which 'none other man had yet lain'. Clearly, the sacred area surrounding the 'green hollow' had such a mystical aura that it was the only appropriate spot to bury an other-worldly figure such as Fergus. But that's only a part of the mystery.

The 'straight road' has mystified commentators for generations. It was not a real road as we would understand it, but a sacred path or route of some kind. And to dowsers the meaning is clear. It is a description of the route of a ley line, sometimes mysteriously referred to as the dragon's path or breath, a route that follows a straight line of mysterious energy running below the surface of the earth; an invisible line, but one that can be detected through dowsing and by people with the sensitivity to be attuned to this natural force. Individuals like the mystic Kentigern. By following this 'invisible road' Kentigern was, perhaps, trying to show his respect for the 'ancient ways' recognising that these mysterious pathways were imbued with a mystical sanctity. The idea of a 'mystical' or 'sacred' route seems to have lasted into medieval times. In Holland, which has enjoyed strong links with Scotland for centuries, earth-mysteries expert Paul Devereux – in *Shamanism and the Mystery Lines* – describes 'the existence of medieval death roads. These old roads had a prescribed width, and were inspected annually by surveyors and travelling magistrates. Dead straight, they converged on cemeteries.' It has been suggested by other experts that these physical roads connected to spiritual straight roads. And these spiritual roads are, quite probably, ley lines, those invisible forces of energy that follow a straight route across the land, but which can be detected by dowsing. The resemblance to Kentigern's journey with Fergus's funeral cart to Glasgow by the 'straight road' is startling. Kentigern's path was not wholly physical; it followed the line of a ley, but it would have ended in a dead-straight section of actual pathway that led to the burial ground. The spirit line probably led to the edge of the Molendinar burn, at the famous 'hollow', so it would be wholly appropriate to build a church at this spot.

More speculatively, it has even been suggested that Kentigern, using his strange abilities, activated  an energy force deep within the spirit line and so generated a mysterious power that raised the funeral train from the ground and carried it as if it was on invisible rails for the thirty-mile journey from Stirling to Glasgow. It has been claimed that the ability to harness this force – knowledge held by the Egyptians and Druids but now lost – explains even greater feats, such as raising the huge stone blocks used to build the pyramids and other ancient structures.

While this may sound like science fiction Kentigern's use of bulls, as described in the accounts of this event, are truly astonishing, as it reveals strong pagan undertones. Long before the arrival of Christianity the bull was regarded as a sacred beast and was still being sacrificed on the Scottish islands up to the end of the eighteenth century much to the disgust, and opposition, of church authorities. We need only think back to ancient civilisations. The Apis bulls of Egypt. The bulls worshipped on Minoan Crete and Greece. Bishop Jocelyn states enigmatically, but quite deliberately, that Fergus was buried in a cemetery where no one other man had been interred before. But had this been in use by pagans for other types of burials? Even for sacred animals like bulls? And what was the fate of the two bulls used by Kentigern? Were they interred with Fergus in some weird ceremony? The Apis bulls of ancient Egypt were buried in their own enormous, underground graveyard. Could this be the type of mysterious cemetery that St Ninian was supposed to have inaugurated? And could this be another mystery of the lower chapel, believed to have been built over the spot where both Kentigern and, by tradition, Fergus lie? Intriguingly, descriptions of Kentigern make him appear more like Merlin the magician than the traditional Christian saint. He possessed strange powers, if the accounts of his life are to be believed. He brought a dead bird back to life and made frozen wood burst into flames by the power of his voice. These were a clear demonstration that his supernatural powers were the equal of those of the Druids and other pagans of the time. It also reveals how fluid religious beliefs were during this era and why St Kentigern had no difficulty in sharing a mystical location with the Druids.

But there are even more unexplained mysteries linked to the 'blue fields'. Close to the sacred area of the cathedral and necropolis lies Dovehill. Buried under years of urban sprawl it can more easily be located by following the line of the Gallowgate to the spot where the streets Little Dovehill and Great Dovehill branch off, indicating its location. Originally known as Dow Hill it is linked to a strange legend. Kentigern was preaching on the low ground, making it difficult for many to see him. Using his extraordinary abilities he miraculously caused the ground on which he was preaching to rise and form a mound. And so was created Dovehill. There's no need to take this at face value. It does not seem that Dovehill is an artificial mound. So it seems likely that it was there when St Kentigern arrived. This event has to be seen as symbolic. Kentigern was raising Dovehill to a special status, marking it as part of the sacred complex around the 'hollow'. It should be noted the 'dove' is a bird particularly associated with early saints such as Columba, and also with the Druids. Tradition also has it that the city's motto, 'Let Glasgow flourish by the preaching of the word', was inspired by the raising of Dovehill. Another indication of how mysticism was intimately connected to the founding of the city.

It is likely that Dovehill formed the southern boundary. Or perhaps it was an attempt to create a sacred hill to counteract the pull of the Druid's centre at Fir Park. The 'sacred fields' of Kentigern's era stretched west to the area known today as Garnethill. But its older name, Summerhill, in use in the distant past, gives a clearer idea of its ancient associations. It was here that the midsummer assembly, known simply as 'the Summerhill', was held. The hill marked the end of the ceremonial walk known as the marches, which began at the Stablegreen where the Bishop's castle stood beside the cathedral. A walk of this type can mark out a boundary of a sacred area or it can have its own mystic significance, as a route where an event of spiritual significance once took place. It seems that through long-forgotten ceremonies like this the tradition of the 'sacred enclosure' was maintained for centuries.

There is a host of Glasgow streets with strange names, which reinforces the idea of the 'sacred centre'. In particular there are two connected thoroughfares, which are a stark reminder of our pagan past. Witch Loan and Bellgrove, once lined with overhanging trees, are likely to have formed part of a sacred pathway. The 'Witch' in Witchgrove speaks for itself, giving a clear indication of its origins. But the 'Bel' part of Bellgrove also provides a clue. It may simply be from the French, bel or belle for beautiful, so in English the 'beautiful grove'. But it could also, quite plausibly, come from Bel, signifying Beltane, an ancient pagan festival, a site where Druids gathered in honour of the Celtic god, Bel. Some suggest that it could have belonged to the cathedral bell ringers, but others have a more sinister suggestion: that 'bel' refers to the fact that the festival of Beltane took place here. This would link neatly with the Witch Loan and Bellgrove thoroughfares. Tradition has it that Witch Loan was under the control of a malevolent entity. A folk memory, it can be guessed, of some pre-Christian site of pagan festivals. Incidentally, present-day Sauchiehall Street lies in the heart of the ancient sacred enclosure. Its name comes from the haugh or meadow where saugh, or willow, trees grew. The willow was a tree with mystical status for Druids. The prolif-eration of these names suggests that the whole area was at one time a focus of other-worldly activity.

But why was this area, located in the heart of modern Glasgow, imbued with a mystical quality? From across Europe evidence has emerged that the countryside is criss-crossed by a strange energy force known as ley lines. Most commonly these have been detected at standing stones and similar prehistoric monuments. They appear to follow a straight route across the country and, according to some dowsers, have an effect on the human mind and body similar to that of electromagnetic energy. In fact, it is believed that ancient structures were erected to mark those spots where ley energy was especially powerful. The area over which Glasgow city centre was built was once covered by standing-stone circles, evidence that the site was regarded as a focus of a powerful energy force. The ancient leys still criss-cross the city. Some lines can be positive and others negative. Some carry a good force, others a bad force. It is said that ghost and poltergeist activity can be linked to ley lines running through a house.

Of course, the idea that in twenty-first-century Scotland a city's development could be influenced by some undefined mystic energy might seem out of place. That may be our attitude in Scotland, but it is not the case everywhere. Austria is not a country that you would associate with outlandish ideas. On the contrary, you feel that if the solid burghers of Switzerland hadn't invented the cuckoo clock the Austrians might well have. They run an orderly and practical society. All the more interesting then that the Austrian city of Innsbruck has been willing to accept the idea that strange forms of energy, called ley lines, run beneath the earth and can have an influence on our lives. In a town park in the heart of medieval Innsbruck stands a well-maintained column. It was a present to the citizens of Innsbruck following a feng shui conference held in the city in 2000. The inscription on the monument reads: 'The energy stone marks the lung point of the City of Innsbruck. An important energy point it improves the energy flow and enhances energy potential in the city of Innsbruck.' The inscription also appears in German and Italian.

Does Glasgow, too, have its lung point, a central focus at

which energies radiating beneath the city are particularly strong? The site where Glasgow cathedral stands would seem an obvious spot, but although those who dowse for ley lines might agree on the general passage of these invisible force lines there might be disagreement on the key locations. These 'lines' are still in place, like an unseen network of electric cables. It's just that we have closed down our senses and no longer consciously tune in to them. But in recent years dowsers have started to unravel the secrets of the past, secrets that explain why Glasgow was chosen as a focus by mystics of whatever religion.

In the 1980s and 1990s Harry Bell mapped out important ley lines crossing the city. He published the results in *Glasgow's Secret Geometry*. These lines, Bell argues, cross certain key and historic sites. One, for example, runs from the necropolis to Castlemilk House and from there to the Lickprivick Tumulus and then to Harelaw cairn. He located several beginning, or terminating, at the necropolis and if the work of other dowsers is taken into account, then this may be the tip of the iceberg. My own dowsing suggests that the hill of the necropolis and the area where the cathedral stands is, in fact, the lung point of Glasgow. It is from here that strong forces of energy radiate outwards. It should be remembered though that in a city the size of Glasgow there may well be lung points spread across the town. Locating these would form a substantial investigation, so we can't be certain that the necropolis–cathedral complex is the key, even if individuals like Kentigern and those before him instinctively recognised it.

We must also consider another key piece of evidence: the strange tales of underground tunnels connecting different parts of Glasgow and their link to the idea of the sacred centre. It is held by ancient tradition that a race of strange entities once inhabited the area on which Rutherglen now stands. These accounts state that they constructed a series of underground tunnels, one of which ran from the cathedral to Rutherglen church, a distance of several miles. Various stories have been linked to the tunnel, the best known being that of the piper who walks into it playing his pipes but does not come back, though the sound of his pipes can be heard from below ground at different spots. We need not take the story of the lost piper at face value, but it may contain a germ of truth. It suggests that there was an extensive network of tunnels, which stretched for some distance. The idea of underground tunnels linking certain areas is an intriguing one. For a start we can dismiss the notion that tunnels were constructed at the time the cathedral and Rutherglen church were built. They went up in different eras and such a construction project would undoubtedly have left more obvious evidence. Surely, if anything, it was the other way round. The two buildings were put up over, or close to, existing tunnels, which, although not directly linked, may have formed a network. They could have been prehistoric in origin, or perhaps a later ritual site, or part of the 'hollow' that made the area widely recognised as a centre of mystery.

Across the city there are tunnels that seem to have no clear purpose, and no particular destination, such as those found beneath the outhouse of the now demolished Broomloan House in Govan. However, certain religious groups – from the Egyptians to the Knights Templar to more recent sects, like black magicians – have used underground sites to carry out their secret rituals. It suggests that for generations the centre of the city attracted those with a mystical frame of mind.

But did this also apply to the dead? Harry Bell, as have dowsers since, located many leys linked to the necropolis. Does this explain why people in the nineteenth century chose this hill as a site for a new graveyard? There seems little doubt that it was selected deliberately because of its mystic association, but were those involved aware of its energy flow? And did they see its mystic associations as energising the spirits of the dead to ease their passage to the other world or facilitate communication with them? This may explain why Fir Park was chosen as the location of the necropolis, even though there were far more obvious sites available. Somehow the hill meant something special to these campaigners. Archaeology may have been in its infancy, but in a way that must have made the myths and traditions of the hill with its Druidic past even more enticing.

The campaign began with an innocuous-sounding booklet entitled *Necropolis Glasguensis*, published in 1831. Its author, John Strang, argued for the conversion of Fir Park, which overlooks the cathedral, into a necropolis, a city of the dead. But why pick such an unappealing location? A rocky hill, steep-sided, uneven, when flat or moderately sloping ground would have been a more obvious choice. It is claimed it was inspired by the famous Père Lachaise cemetery in Paris, but a visit there reveals the terrain to be in stark contrast to the site selected for the necropolis. But Strang's idea of what the necropolis would be like is anything but straightforward. He pictured it as a place where the dead would come to life again, where the citizens of this world would be able to commune with the spirits of the departed. He wrote enthusiastically of Egyptian burial customs, especially the practice of sitting a deceased relative, wrapped in bandages for preservation, at the dinner table in the belief that by doing so they showed respect and would be able to communicate with their dead kin.

Strang's obsession with a site that would allow cave-like vaults for the dead supports the idea that he had much more than a simple graveyard in mind. It was in such a spot that Jesus of Nazareth was resurrected. It was in the interior of a pyramidical vault that the Egyptian dead would walk again. Strang strongly condemned the protection of graves by iron railings, even though the practice had been adopted to protect against grave robbers, and wanted them banned from the necropolis. He clearly believed in a cemetery in which the barriers between the living and the dead would be minimal, so that neither would operate within entirely separate spheres, an idea that the Druids and Kentigern would instinctively have recognised as in tune with the aura of the place. Can the necropolis, the city of the dead, really be seen as little more than an ordinary graveyard when it possesses such strange monuments as the Egyptian Vaults, and the Facade? And where the statue to John Knox now stands at the spot on which the pagan worshippers of Sol, the sun god, once gathered. Is it simply speculation to suggest that Strang and those who supported him chose this site because it was close to the mystical heart of Glasgow? Did they, consciously or unconsciously, appreciate that this particular area radiates a special aura?

Another factor to bear in mind is that outlying sites were once part of a mystic network. The land occupied for several centuries by the ancient church of Inchinnan – lying on the southern side of the Clyde close to the spot where it is met by the waters of the Black Cart – was once a sacred site linked to the mystic heartland dominated by the cathedral. Exactly what their relationship might be is unclear, but the site was taken over by St Conal, a disciple of Kentigern. And to emphasise the link between the two sites, Inchinnan then came under the control of the Knights Templar sometime in the twelfth century. It is possible that a holy straight path, like that St Kentigern followed from Stirling to Glasgow, connected the 'green hollow' to Inchinnan. It is no longer possible to determine exactly the route this followed, but dowsing has indicated that a ley line still links the two sites. Most probably the 'sacred route' followed the same course above ground. It is likely that the knowledge of where leys ran encouraged the settlement of these, and other, sites. One ley, for example, runs from the cathedral to St Enoch's Square. It is said that St Enoch, mother of St Kentigern, set up a sanctuary here with a well whose waters she blessed and which, thereafter, had the power to cure a variety of illnesses.

Mystic sites are not confined to one country and it has been speculated that Glasgow is part of an underground conspiracy, a secret web of hidden knowledge that linked individuals across Europe, but has only recently come to light. The French hilltop village of Rennes-le-Chateau, deep in Cathar country in southern France, has attracted considerable attention because of certain unexplained puzzles. It has been connected to a network of mysteries linking the Knights Templar, the Holy Grail, the Vatican and the alleged descendants of Jesus who, according to alternative historians, was married to Mary Magdalene, who bore him several children. The mystery of Rennes-le-Chateau (woven into the best-selling novel, *The Da Vinci Code*) is that Berenger Sauniere – the priest from 1885 to 1917 of this tiny, and, at the time, remote and impoverished community – spent the equivalent today of £1 million on improving his small chapel and constructing a strange, walled garden. There has never been any reasonable explanation as to how he acquired such vast sums. The suggestion is that during renovation of the chapel grounds he discovered strange documents that showed Jesus was married and had children. It is said he either sold these documents or his silence was bought by the Vatican. But can any of this be connected to Scotland? Or Glasgow in particular? On the walls of Sauniere's house can still be seen fading wallpaper covered in thistles. Does this represent a connection? Here too are glass windows depicting bright red, or bloodstained, hearts, similar to the heart motif adopted by the Douglas family and to be found in Rosslyn chapel and in Glasgow cathedral. Can we read anything into this? Or is it just coincidence? There is, however, a more direct visual link, which may or may not be significant, but is undeniably intriguing. In the Blacader aisle of Glasgow cathedral you will find a carved figure of the face of the Devil, painted red, and above it, standing almost on Satan's head, another figure dressed in a blue smock. Though admittedly on a larger scale and with a full body, you can see at Rennes-le-Chateau an ochre figure of the Devil with, above it, standing almost on its head, four figures, one clearly dressed in a blue smock. The similarity of these figures in buildings a thousand or so miles apart is astonishing.

It has been claimed that the devil figure at Rennes-le-Chateau represents a tradition, an idea of some kind that formed a secret code connecting individuals across Europe. A view, expressed behind closed doors, that Christian belief, as presented by religious leaders, was not the whole story. It may be that ancient traditions, especially those of the Druids, played a larger part in the formation of Christianity than has ever been officially admitted.

This theory is given added weight by Glasgow's 'green hollow', and the sacred area that once surrounded it, which still form the heart of the city. It was an area that over thousands of years attracted mystics of all kinds; individuals who understood that the area operated as a twilight zone in which different dimensions met and interacted. It was a fitting site to consider hiding the Holy Grail, whether or not it was carried out in practice. In recent centuries, for whatever reason, the mystic land at the heart of Glasgow was ignored, then forgotten and built over. But as dowsers have shown, the invisible energy known as ley lines still runs through the city, and their most powerful focus remains, as it was in Kentigern's time, at the city's lung point, the mysterious green hollow from which Glasgow takes its name.

# 3

# Ghosts and Phantoms

Ancient buildings seem the natural places to meet a ghost. Their age and character make it more likely that, in the past, some tragic event has taken place. One from which the spirit of a deceased person can never quite escape. But why do spectres haunt less-traditional spots? Places like Glasgow's transport museum. Or a snooker hall. And even Glasgow airport. There doesn't seem to be a straightforward explanation. Ghosts appear whenever and wherever the time and place meet their fancy. Or, perhaps, when a portal between this dimension and the next unexpectedly opens.

Few historic sites escape their attention. Although Glasgow has expanded and developed through the centuries, building on top of demolished segments of the ancient city, enough remains to provide us with a remarkable insight into the nature of the super-natural. Bedlay castle, which overlooks the busy A80 at Chryston, has a rich tradition as a focus for ghostly activity. Apparitions were seen long before the existing building – which itself dates from the sixteenth century – was erected. In 1175 a manor house, now demolished, was built here as an official home for the bishops of Glasgow. It is claimed that the ghost of one former resident has been haunting the site for centuries. The spectre first appeared as long ago as 1350, the year in which legend has it that John Cameron, bishop of Glasgow, died in mysterious circumstances. He was found in a nearby loch, floating face down. It was suspected that he had been murdered.

However, if the ghost really is that of Cameron then it can't date from 1350. He, in fact, held the office from 1426 to 1446, a century after the start of the alleged haunting. John Cameron may be a likely character for the ghost though. He was a controversial figure who was for a time excommunicated by the pope for various alleged crimes, though he was later forgiven and died as bishop of Glasgow. All of which might raise questions about Cameron, but doesn't directly link him to the Bedlay ghost. Intriguingly, however, a bishop did die in 1350. This was William de Deyn, but he was the bishop of Aberdeen and there is nothing to connect him to either Bedlay or Glasgow. It does, however, add a curious twist to the story.

During the nineteenth century sightings of the Bedlay ghost became more frequent, but this spectre was believed to be that of James Campbell of Petershill who, having bought the estate, built a mausoleum in the castle grounds. After Campbell's death the mausoleum became the focus for spirit manifestations although ghostly figures were also encountered in the surrounding woods. So intense was the spectral activity that in the 1880s a group of clergymen were invited into the castle to exorcise whatever was haunting the area. According to a report of the time they emerged from the castle with 'sweat running down their brows'. They certainly didn't succeed in releasing any evil linked to the place, or if they did, whatever had been haunting the building eventually returned. In 1969 an antiques dealer moved into Bedlay castle with his wife and two young children. Not long after they arrived both daughters claimed to have seen a ghost. On several occasions women visiting felt an invisible presence touch their hair, a typical occurrence when a spirit is trying to make contact. The sounds of footsteps pacing up and down the hall were also heard. Witnesses who encountered the spectre in the 1970s described a large, bearded figure dressed in clerical robes. Could this have been the ghost of John Cameron? Or was it the spirit of some unknown person linked to the area? Perhaps it was that of the body found in the loch whose identity over the years somehow became mixed up with that of the Glasgow bishop.

When James Campbell's mausoleum was eventually dismantled and moved to Lambhill cemetery the manifestations continued at the new site. Sightings were reported of luminous figures that walked up to the mausoleum and then simply disappeared.

A castle can be linked with many deaths so may well 'lock in' unhappy spirits. But less clear is why a location like the Royale snooker club in Rutherglen should be visited by spectres of the dead. In the 1990s the club was host to various strange phenomena, as an investigation by Arlene Russo, editor of *Bite Me* magazine, revealed. On one occasion staff witnessed a bizarre transformation take place while watching a security monitor. The face of an unknown old man with white hair suddenly appeared from nowhere on the screen. As people watched the man's hair grew darker. His face became younger. Though he appeared to be lying in a coffin the mysterious image seemed to be running backwards through time. The body slowly transformed into that of a young person.

But was this weird event connected to the appearance of slime-formed footprints on steps leading down to the cellar? This storage area seemed to be haunted by the ghost of an unidentified man. Staff who went down there sensed his presence. Some even caught a glimpse of him out of the corner of an eye. Others claimed that he gave off a strange, disturbing smell. However, when people tried to look directly at the apparition it vanished. On another occasion an employee was cleaning glasses when he saw the image of a man in the mirror behind the bar. He was dressed in a three-piece suit. When he turned around the man had disappeared, but he caught sight of a dark shadow without a solid body moving, like a living being, stealthily across the floor. Customers reported that lights and televisions would switch themselves on and off. A psychic who visited the club reported that there were many spirits present, some of an evil nature that were being kept under control in another dimension by a priest dressed in black robes. This sounds similar to the man dressed in robes reported at Bedlay castle. Could this mean that there exists, in another dimension, a whole class of strange beings sharing the same characteristics? Several years later in 2007 the club was still the subject of ghostly visitations. Psychics had made contact with former members, whom, it appears, still enjoyed the atmosphere of the snooker club, even though they had passed into the spirit world.

Ghosts often seem involved in some way with the places they are seen. But are ghosts so attracted to their former possessions that they would return to our world to reclaim their property? That may explain the disturbances in 1999 at the Auctioneers, a city-centre pub housed in a two-hundred-year-old building just a stone's throw from Glasgow's bustling George Square. The manager, Michael – whom I interviewed for my 'X Files' column in the *Evening Times* – had reported a series of unexplained events that shook both staff and regulars. Michael had been in charge for only a few months at the time the disturbances started, but he was aware that the pub had a history of paranormal events. He explained:

There have always been strange incidents linked with the building, especially unexplained noises. One of the staff was in the cellar sorting out stock when he heard doors banging. It sounded weird and he knew that there was no one else around to make the noise. But it is the sightings that have really unnerved people. One of our chefs, who had just recently started, was on his lunch break, having a coffee on the stairs. Out of nowhere a girl appeared and ran along the corridor. There had been children in for lunches that day because this place has both a bar and diner, so the chef jumped up to go after the girl to tell her that she shouldn't be down there, but by this time she'd vanished into thin air. There was no way that she could have got out because the doors are all alarmed and nothing went off. To get back up to the diner she would have had to pass the chef and clearly didn't. The chef came running up to tell us. He'd got the fright of his life. He said that she had a Victorian dress on and was about thirteen or fourteen years old. The oddest thing was that she was wearing clogs. It was the sound of these on the floor that the chef thought he had heard first.

The pub had been running for three years when the incidents took place, but the area it occupied included much of the original building and decor. It used to be the auction rooms of a company that sold household goods. Could the dead either have resented the sale of their possessions or, alternatively, had such a strong sentimental attachment to them that they couldn't bear to be parted? There is certainly a long tradition that a spirit can live within or be connected to a particular object and that by bringing an object into a house you can unwittingly bring in a dead person's spirit. But that doesn't explain why the spirits would continue to hang around the pub long after the auctioneers had closed. A more likely explanation is that the spirits were linked to the area and that a member of staff was unknowingly opening up to allow the spirits in. As a member of staff put it, 'We are refurbishing in a few months but we don't want to disturb any ghosts even more.'

Michael explained to me:

Several others have felt there's a strange atmosphere about the place. The head chef has been downstairs and felt a presence. My own feeling is that maybe there's a spirit here that is trying to get out. When I've been in the building I've heard footsteps and heard the floorboards creaking. So I can vouch that odd things are going on. Not long after the chef saw that young girl there was a strange incident involving a customer in the downstairs toilet area. He felt the room go extremely cold and had the feeling that an invisible presence was there looking at him. He put it down to imagination but then felt someone breathing down his neck. He came back up in a state and left without finishing his drink. Believe me, a journey to the toilets is an experience in itself. Several of our female staff are unhappy going to the toilets on their own. And the ice machine is down there too, which means a nerve-racking trip for someone.

Apparently, there had been a murder a few years earlier in a nearby street. Although it may be tempting to link this tragic event to the haunting there was no evidence that the victim's spirit was connected to the sightings.

Mhairi, head chef at the time, had first-hand experience of the events:

I saw the little girl with my own eyes so I can vouch for the sightings. She's a young thing, about thirteen or fourteen I would say. She was wearing a long, grey dress with a white overall. She definitely looked Victorian. She just walked by me. A young type of face and a very slender-looking lass. Quite small. Her hair is down to her shoulders. I don't think that she is aware of our presence. I'm not sure what she is doing here, but I do have the feeling that she is trying to get out. She didn't make any noise when I saw her. As far as I know every time she's been seen, she comes from the office area and goes along the corridor. The doors down there bang shut and if she was a real person we would definitely hear her. I believe there were old tobacco merchants here so it could be one of the girls from there. The spirit must be coming through very strongly. That's why I saw her. The day the other chef saw the girl he got a real fright. His hair was standing on end and he was shaking.

Top Scottish medium Katrina McNab commented on the incidents at the time, saying: 'Doing up the bar shouldn't have any effect on the ghost. Maybe in the past people were buried where the building stands. That might explain the disturbance. Or the spirit might be linked to someone who works there.'

It is hard sometimes to understand why a dead person's ghost would become so attached to a location. But, in other cases, it's more obvious. Actors put so much emotion into a performance that it is understandable the spirits of dead performers are found wandering the corridors in which they experienced long-forgotten triumphs or died an actor's 'death' on stage. But can that explain every reported sighting? The Citizens theatre in Gorbals Street, built in 1878, is said to be haunted by a green lady, a front-of-house manager who committed suicide by jumping from the upper circle. This ghost has been around for a long time as the incident, by tradition, took place in the nineteenth century soon after the theatre opened. However, the apparition was seen within the last twenty years, witnessed by a member of staff who was working on the stage set when the phantom suddenly appeared in the upper circle.

In fact Glasgow's theatres seem to be a hotspot of ghostly activity. The Ramshorn theatre, once a church, is haunted by a woman called Edie. She has been seen in an area that is now the site of the toilet block, but was previously the minister's vestry. Strange footsteps have been heard, along with overpowering smells. An explanation for the haunting of the Ramshorn could be connected to the construction of the present church in 1842. At that time Ingram Street was made into a thoroughfare and as a result was extended over the ancient graveyard where the old church stood. Graves were paved over though it is unclear if the bodies of the dead were moved from their resting places. Whether they were or not, psychics are convinced that disturbing the dead in this way, by some reverberation through the ethereal atmosphere or other dimensions, stirs up spirit activity. It was also a site favoured by resurrectionists (men who dug up freshly buried corpses to sell to the medical profession) though given the passage of time since 1842 it is unlikely to be the whole explanation. This area was recognised as a mystic site thousands of years ago and it may be that the appearance of phantoms long predated the construction of the church.

As much as pubs, theatres seem to attract the spirits of the dead. At the Theatre Royal, built in 1876 and now the home of Scottish Opera, the ghosts of two different spirits have been regularly witnessed. The phantom of a woman has been seen looking over the balcony from the front row of the circle. Unexplained door banging and the sounds of someone sighing are said to be linked to her appearance. The spectre is believed to be the ghost of an aspiring actress who became so frustrated by her lack of success that she threw herself to her death from the same spot where the apparition now appears. The woman was so desperate to enter the acting profession that she would take on any menial job just to be involved with the theatre. The hoped-for big break never materialised; hence her tragic end. The theatre, however, is said to be the haunt of a second ghost, that of a fireman who died fighting a blaze in the building. He has appeared in the orchestra pit on a number of occasions.

However, in terms of sheer numbers these theatres are outdone by the Pavilion, which has three ghosts. Tommy Morgan – a well-known comic of his era, who died in 1961 – had his ashes scattered on the roof of the theatre. His ghost has been seen not only in the upper part of the building, near where his ashes were released, but also where every performer wishes to be – close to the stage. In the auditorium witnesses have reported encountering a female apparition. But as well as ghosts there has been direct physical evidence that odd incidents are happening. Piano music has been heard echoing round the building, believed to be the work of an invisible pianist from beyond the grave. Various items have been moved and objects have disappeared, and then reappeared, with no obvious explanation.

But theatres can be the scene of real, as well as fictional, tragedy. In 1782 a theatre opened in Dunlop Street in the city centre, which attracted the stars of the time including Jenny Lind. In 1849, however, during a performance a rumour swept through the audience that fire had broken out. It was a false alarm, but in the stampede for the exits several dozen people died. The theatre eventually closed and St Enoch station was built on the site then replaced by the St Enoch shopping centre, which encompasses most of Dunlop Street. But does the fate of the 1849 theatre disaster still haunt the area and account for the running figures with a strange glow that have been reported? It may be coincidence, but it could explain the old-fashioned dress worn by the apparitions.

Oddly, cinema hauntings are less numerous, or maybe they are simply not reported. The Old Waverley Picture House on Moss Side Road, later the Waverley Shawlands EMI bingo and social club, was haunted by a one-time projectionist, whose ghost was encountered by several people. The spectre was assumed to have been that of the projectionist because of the area in which the ghost was seen. But there's been no explanation as to why he should have been so attached to the place. Was it sheer devotion to the job? This haunting can be compared with that at the former Glen cinema in Paisley, the remains of which lie hidden behind a furniture store. Given the appalling events in which many children lost their lives in a stampede for the exits it's not surprising that staff in adjoining premises report hearing unexplained footsteps and shrieking voices and find objects appearing and disappearing.

Ghosts often appear as transparent phantoms, vague outlines through which the background of a room can be seen. Sometimes they look as solid as any normal person. But it is a rare ghost that not only looks solid, but also talks and interacts with the living. Are they truly ghosts? Or solid bodies transported to earth from another dimension? What then can their purpose be? The events documented in the following incident were originally reported by investigator Terence Whitaker, an authority on haunting with a national reputation. He was given the details by a railway porter and wrote a lengthy account in his book, *Scotland's Ghosts and Apparitions*. The case raises a number of issues about the nature of ghosts and the way that reports enter the public domain. It is a complex and lengthy incident that deserves close examination. In the early part of the twentieth century James McLeary, a junior doctor, was making his way from the Western Infirmary to Glasgow Central station. In 1913 smoke-free fuel lay decades in the future so the heart of the city was blanketed in thick smog. The young medic found it harder than he thought to find his destination. Out of the fog a stranger appeared and offered to take him there as he was heading the same way. Eventually, they reached the station and having had a chat discovered they were catching the same train. They sat together still talking as the train pulled out of the station. McLeary's new acquaintance told him of an incident he had been involved in two years previously on a train heading out from the same platform, on a similar foggy night. As he sat alone in a compartment another passenger had jumped in. McLeary's companion told him that on that night he was carrying several hundred pounds in a briefcase and was immediately wary of the sudden new arrival. Caution that was quickly proved correct when the man took out a knife and demanded that he hand over the money. A struggle followed. McLeary naturally assumed his companion had beaten off his attacker, but was shocked when he replied: 'No, he stabbed me in the heart and killed me.' He then immediately disappeared.

The ghost that looks solid, and even talks, is not unknown. There are several stories of the phantom hitchhiker, the man or woman picked up by a passing motorist who mysteriously disappears before the intended destination is reached. However, the length of time and complexity of the McLeary incident marks it as one of the most bizarre of all such encounters. It is claimed that the incident is linked to a real event. In February 1911, Patrick Noon, a twenty-seven-year-old warehouseman from Govan, was executed at Barlinnie prison. He had been found guilty of murdering businessman George Ferguson on the Glasgow to London Euston train. Mr Ferguson's body was discovered when the train stopped at Motherwell.

It is not clear, however, why George Ferguson reappeared as

he did. Though this is a documented incident, it is more complex than most, and more extensive than the brief summary I've given, involving prolonged communication between Ferguson and McLeary after their meeting and on the train. You might expect there to be a motive for Ferguson's extended reappearance from the grave. But, apart from the fact that it happened on a foggy night, there is no obvious link between the two events. There is not even evidence that McLeary's encounter was played out on the anniversary of Ferguson's death. I should add that I have been unable to discover further information about Patrick Noon or the crime that led to his execution. It is possible that several events have become entangled within an undoubtedly strange incident. It has to be said though that in most cases involving strange phenomena no real reason for the bridging of different worlds can be pinned down. It just seems to happen.

As events in Glasgow's transport museum appear to show. Incidents in the museum were brought to public attention by security guard Bill Mutch; incidents that I covered in some depth for the *Evening Times*. Following a phone conversation in May 1998 I met up with Bill in the museum's impressive entrance hall. He struck me as an intelligent and thoughtful man, who was determined to let people know about the events he had witnessed. His account shows that, for whatever reasons, the museum was a hotbed of supernatural activity. He took me on a tour of the exhibits and explained the phenomena he had experienced. He told me about the first thing he had seen:

A pale-blue wave coming from the top of the tearoom, going down through it then over the engine exhibits before it vanished. It changed the colour of the lights as it moved. I also saw a ball of blue lights, which travelled over the display area upstairs. It was about five-feet across and I could see right through it. I was videoing at the time, but nothing came out on the film. It was really strange.

The colour blue is often seen as an indication, psychics tell us, that a door has been opened to other worlds.

It is said that the transport museum was used as a mortuary after the Clydebank blitz, but there is no evidence specifically to link the phantoms to those tragic events of 1941. It may, however, have generated more spirit activity. But the range of phenomena suggests there is a deeper, more extensive mystery at work. Had the museum been, unknowingly, built on a sacred spot, which allowed a portal to other dimensions to be opened? The sheer range of incidents reported by Bill Mutch suggests that something strange was going on. Bill, who was often in the museum late at night, heard the voices of children screaming beside the old steam train kept in the museum. Was there a train crash linked to the engines? Bill also heard footsteps following him when he went on patrol, though he knew no one else was in the museum at the time. 'They stopped when I stopped,' Bill explained, 'and started when I started. There was also a jingling noise. Later I learned that a driver of an old-style train had somehow managed to hang himself with his horse reins. I am sure this was the ghost that followed me.'

Disturbing though these events were, Bill Mutch believed that the ethereal atmosphere created in the museum led him to develop healing abilities. Bill said that when a workmate complained of a painful shoulder he held his hands above the sore area. Bill reported, 'She felt an instant heat in her shoulder and on the back of her neck. My hands felt as if there were pins firing from them, like a magnetic charge.' One thing that psychics have noted is that no matter how widespread a haunting may seem within a building there is always one location that is the focus. And from which the whole environment of a place may be affected. A worm hole to another world? Bill Mutch had no doubt that as far as the museum was concerned the most intense spectral activity was centred on the specially recreated 1930s street with its cinema, shops, pub and underground station. Bill reported hearing heavy footsteps walking down the street when he knew he was patrolling on his own. On one occasion he heard the sound of a man limping, dragging his leg along the ground. He also claimed to have seen 'a tall, dark shadow go into the model toyshop'.

According to Mutch a strange energy radiated from the mural at the end of the street. He described feeling 'how a form of energy from the picture went right through my body'. The centre of activity was, for Bill, the cinema: 'It always feels cold in there and the door opens and closes by itself.' And Bill sensed that there could be something evil involved. He described how a friend was with him in the cinema when a row of seats, which had all been in the up position, suddenly crashed down in unison. A while later the friend was killed in an accident. Bill felt that this incident was somehow connected to his friend's death. A warning from another domain? Bill also felt that his friend was trying to contact him from time to time and thought he heard his voice calling to him as he walked through the museum.

Filled with ageing exhibits, many of which may have been involved in some tragic story, it is understandable that a museum may attract the spirits of the deceased. But an airport – modern, contemporary and high tech – is the last place you would expect to encounter a phantom. But even in this unlikely place you cannot escape the clash with other dimensions. On 15 June 1995 pilot Bob Hambleton was preparing to fly a cargo plane from Glasgow airport to Moscow. As he was heading through the concourse at around 2.45 p.m. to get to his plane he spotted a friend, Robert Macleod, coming through the doors. They had previously flown together for several years for Loganair, piloting planes on routes between Glasgow and the Scottish islands. They had not, however, been in touch for a while as Macleod had moved to a new company and Hambleton's career had taken him to other parts of Scotland. Bob Hambleton was struck by the fact that his friend did not look at all well, though he chatted amicably for several minutes. He did think it odd, however, when MacLeod didn't shake his hand when offered it. Eventually, his pal glanced at his watch and told Hambleton that he would have to go as he had 'a plane to catch'. By the time Hambleton had bent down to pick up his bags and stood up again his friend was nowhere to be seen.

The following day, although one puzzle was answered, a number of new questions were raised. Bob's attention was drawn to a report in *The Scotsman*. It was an obituary of his friend who had died, it read, four days before in hospital following an operation. The obituary headed, 'Captain Robert D. Macleod', and accompanied by a photograph of the deceased, appeared in *The Scotsman* on Wednesday, 14 June 1995. A date of 11 June was given as the date of Captain Macleod's death, which it appears, followed an illness, so Bob Hambleton's friend could certainly not have been walking through Glasgow airport terminal on 15 June or, in fact, at any time in the first few weeks of June. Macleod was a well-known figure in Scottish aviation circles, as the lengthy obituary testifies. It confirms that he was 'brought up in Stornoway', carried out his training at British Airways College in Hamble and, in 1981, 'became a flying instructor at Dundee'. He then took his first job 'as a commercial pilot with Loganair' and was based in Glasgow. This period of his life lasted till the late 1980s and it must have been during this time that he and Bob Hambleton became acquainted. At the end of the Eighties Macleod 'took a command . . . flying Islander aircraft throughout the Shetland Isles'. The fact that Macleod was a well-known figure and that his obituary was published with a photograph suggests that even though Bob had not seen Robert for a while he was unlikely to have been mistaken with his identification. If Bob Hambleton did indeed meet Robert Macleod on 15 June then he had just failed to shake hands with a ghost. A further odd twist was that a flight for Stornoway was scheduled to depart at 3 p.m. and Robert Macleod was a native of Lewis. Does this explain his comment to Hambleton that he had 'a plane to catch'? Was Robert Macleod's ghost so tied to his island roots that he could not bear to leave them behind?

On the face of it, the same bond is unlikely to exist between a hotel and its guests, but hotels, in fact, are a regular haunt of spirits from other worlds. The upmarket surroundings of the Hilton hotel in the city centre seem an unlikely venue for ghostly activity, but in the 1990s it experienced a sudden burst of other-worldly phenomena. It was claimed that guests and staff saw a woman sporting a blue dress walking through the bar who suddenly disappeared. Even stranger was the sighting of a man surrounded by a white, glowing aura that appeared to one witness as if he was drenched in wet concrete. This led to speculation that the spectre was that of a notorious Glasgow gangster who disappeared in the 1960s and whose body was never found. It was rumoured that his corpse had been buried in the foundations of the Kingston Bridge and so his appearance in the Hilton, situated close to the M8 motorway, was 'proof' of the location of his body. A more likely explanation, however, is that the phantom was surrounded by ectoplasm – a mysterious, thick, white substance that appears to allow a more solid manifestation of a spirit. To those unfamiliar with it, ectoplasm could easily give the appearance of wet concrete enveloping a spirit body.

An explanation put forward for these events was that the hotel had been built close to the site of an ancient graveyard located in the Anderston area. When the Kingston Bridge was built the remains of the dead were taken away and reburied. It was also claimed that when the site was being developed workmen discovered, in August 1990, a human skull and bones near to where the Hilton now stands. It could be that the spirits of the graveyard corpses had remained attached to the spot, but some of the incidents reported by staff at the Hilton suggest an entity simply out to annoy. Female employees were frightened by wolf whistles made when they were on their own in the Raffles bar. On other occasions staff claimed that they had seen 'glasses moving by themselves, and stools falling over'. They had also been disturbed by loud voices when the room was empty.

More direct was the experience of Alison Brooke at the Old

Shawfields hotel who, in the 1970s, claimed to have heard foot-steps approaching her bedroom door, followed by a glowing light moving through the room. The air suddenly went cold and she thought she could make out the face of a woman as the white ball passed by and travelled straight through the outside wall.

Events at the Hilton and Old Shawfields were simply a more recent manifestation of a long line of ghostly encounters experi-enced by Glasgow hotel guests through the years. A much older incident, reported by ghost-hunter Elliott O'Donnell, involved Hely Browne, a well-known musical actor of more than a century ago. The hotel room Browne booked at the last minute was on the small side, which made the events that unfolded even stranger. He was awoken during his first night by a loud crash and decided since he'd been disturbed to pour a drink of juice from a bottle he had left on the mantelpiece. As he groped his way round the room in the dark he suddenly felt he was in a different place. His bed had disappeared and as he felt for it to get his bearings his hands brushed against a length of rope. It turned out to be a noose suspended from the ceiling. Unable to move because his whole body was paralysed he felt the rope fall around his neck and then tighten as he was lifted off his feet. He tried to scream, but instead passed out. Then suddenly everything was back to normal and his bed could be found exactly where he expected it to be. Nervously, and with the light now on, he lay down to get some sleep. When he came to it was morning and everything was normal although he was out of bed and lying on the floor. There were no marks on his neck to prove that his experience had been a genuine event though, at the time, it had seemed all too real. The following night, lying awake, he experienced a vision in which his brother's face appeared and told him that he had died some weeks before. Hely Browne had not yet heard the news as his brother lived abroad, but the following day a letter arrived confirming the ghost's words. Had some psychic message been passed from the world beyond? If not it seems a remarkable coincidence. Yet would a brother terrify his sibling in such a frightening way? And for what purpose? It sometimes seems that the universe plays tricks to make a point in the most bizarre of ways. Ghosts and the spirit world do not appear to obey any rules, contrary to what many psychics claim.

Perhaps because confronting a spectre in a closed space can be an intensely disturbing experience most reported hauntings seem to occur in a room inside a home, castle, pub or other building. However, ghosts can be encountered anywhere, even in the open air. Helen from Cardonald related how, at the age of nine, she got lost and found herself being followed by a black-coated spectre, which floated in midair. Wandering for several hours, Helen was eventually found and taken to the police station. Although she explained to the woman who found her about the 'strange man', no one else had seen him. Helen described the 'lovely glow' that the figure emanated, 'which lit up where I was running'. She adds: 'When I turned round he was always there, no matter how fast I ran.' Astonishingly, the figure appeared around a year later to tell Helen that he could not come a second time to help her. Though ghosts are usually regarded as a frightening apparition, in this case it was more like the appearance of a 'guardian spirit'. Those spirits of the departed who mediums claim are always on hand to watch us.

But are some events simply destined to happen? Late at night a railway station, especially on the underground, can appear an eerie spot. You might expect such a spot to play on the imagination, but the ghostly encounters reported have been too similar to be ascribed to a sense of unease. They are also connected to particular locations, suggesting that we are dealing with a genuine phenomenon. The Shields Road underground station is haunted by the apparition known as the 'grey lady', believed to be the spirit of a woman hit by a train after she had fallen on to the railway line, an accident that took place as long ago as 1922. Workmen repairing the track claimed to have heard echoing footsteps when no one should have been there and the outline of shimmering figures have been glimpsed. The section between Shields Road and Kinning

Park is reputedly the focus of ghostly activity, and over the years the spectre has been encountered many times. Apparently, she died in July and it is said this is the month in which she usually appears, which means that sightings at other times of the year may be of a different ghost entirely.

My investigation has confirmed that the Shields Road haunting is based on a real event and I can reveal the name of the 'grey lady'. On Saturday, 22 July 1922 thirty-year-old Mrs Adelaide Carpenter of 359 Maryhill Road and her two-year-old daughter, Ethel, fell onto the railway line just as a train was coming into the station. It is not clear if this was an accident or a deliberate attempt at suicide. The only witness to the event was the stationmaster, Robert McIntosh. According to details in the *Glasgow Herald*, McIntosh 'was seated on a stool in the middle of the platform with his back to the stairway. Hearing a scream, McIntosh turned and saw the woman and the child lying on the rail on the inner-circle line.' He tried to stop the incoming train, but it braked too late and went over Adelaide and Ethel. The little girl survived, however, and was pulled free. She had suffered only bruising and broken fingers. Adelaide was alive for at least half an hour after the fall, but by the time she was pulled free was dead. A fractured skull was recorded as the cause of death. The fact that Adelaide alone died might explain why she, and not her daughter, haunt the line. It would be sad to think that her spirit was searching for little Ethel on the anniversary of her own death. Perhaps it is this quest that pulls her back every July.

The city's railways, in fact, are the scene of a surprising number of apparitions. Hillhead underground station is the location for an occasional appearance from a singing ghost. She has been seen late at night or early in the morning, wearing an evening dress. Witnesses claim to hear her singing before she disappears into a tunnel. Who this ghost is and why she haunts the underground is a complete mystery. In 1991 James Montgomery was alone at Carntyne station at ten in the morning when he noticed a young woman about to come on to the platform. Montgomery described her as in her twenties, just over five-feet tall, with long, brown hair. She was wearing a duffel coat and carrying a duffel bag. There was no click of heels on the ground as she moved and he had the distinct impression that she was gliding rather than walking, though it didn't at that moment strike him as strange. Then the train arrived, but the woman seemed to be making no effort to move faster to get to it and James turned to urge her to hurry up. But she had disappeared and though he looked up and down the platform there was no sign of her. And there was no way that she could have got on the train before him or done so without him noticing. Afterwards, James realised that he had not seen the woman's feet. It was as if they had sunk into the platform, a phenomenon sometimes associated with ghosts, which leads to the conclusion that the entity was alive when the ground on which they appeared was at a different level. It turned out that some years before a woman around the age James had described had committed suicide on the line leading to the station although there is no way of knowing whether his sighting and the suicide are connected.

It is unusual to find ghosts linked to a new structure, but why should mere age make a building haunted? Is it simply that more people have passed through its doors? Provan Hall in Auchinlea Park, overlooking the Fort shopping centre, was built in the fifteenth century and was once owned by the bishops of Glasgow. Dating from more lawless times it is not a surprise to learn that a spectre, the White Lady, has been reported in the grounds. But, unusually, this is one ghost who also speaks. She has been heard calling plaintively for her son. It is believed that the White Lady is the apparition of a woman who was killed with her child in a first-floor bedroom. Oddly, no one has reported seeing the ghost of the dead boy. And it would be a tragic twist if the two had been separated in death, his spirit having gone to the land beyond while hers remains earthbound, forever searching for her lost lad till someone can release her. Provan Hall is one of those places that attracts more than one ghost. The apparition of Reston Mathers, the last owner of the property, has been encountered on a number of occasions.

Interestingly, Annfield house, which once stood at the top of Bellgrove in the city centre, was also said to be haunted by a white lady. It has been suggested that apparitions of this nature are often guardians of holy wells. There were certainly many wells close by at one time though no evidence that Bellgrove's white lady was the 'spirit protector' of one.

Another long-standing ghost used to be encountered in Castlemilk. Best known today as one of Europe's largest local-authority housing estates, Castlemilk was, in fact, named after a castle that survived until the 1960s, used in its last few years as a children's home, at which time it was demolished. But the ghost dates from many years before that. Both a white and a green lady have been reported in the grounds in which the building once stood. The focus of activity centred round a bridge running over the nearby burn. A phantom soldier was also seen charging up to the door of the castle on a phantom horse. It was reputed to be the ghost of Captain William Stirling Stuart, a cavalryman, whom, the tradition goes, made a famous gallop to report Wellington's victory after the Battle of Waterloo in 1815. It is simply not clear, however, why this event should have been re-enacted here. It seems likely that the apparition was that of some unidentified or long-forgotten rider who had an association with the place and that this has become mixed up with dramatic events from elsewhere.

Although most ghosts appear harmless some exude evil. Cowden Mansion, which stood at the end of Great Western Road, gained a bad reputation as a haunted residence. In the grounds lay an area where it was said no grass would grow as it had been the site for strange rituals, rituals that had disturbed the sanctity of the spot forever. The building itself, home for several generations to families with money to burn, was haunted by the spirit of a visitor who had allegedly developed a conscience over various terrible acts he had been involved in. He expected that when he 'went over' he would literally descend into a life of torment. In a deranged state of mind he had the fire in his bedroom stoked up and stood in his nightshirt in front of the flames so that he could experience the fate that awaited him. He died later that night in suspicious circumstances, though whether murder was involved no one can be sure. For many years after, for as long as the house stood, his spectre reappeared in the room when the fire was lit, staring in awe at the blazing coals. Truly a ghost from hell.

The spectre has disappeared along with the house, which suggests that some ghosts are not necessarily always with us. Like that of Robert Dreghorn, who inherited a fortune from his father, a wealthy timber merchant and the first man to use a four-wheeled carriage in the city. The son was also left an impressive mansion in Great Clyde Street, which became a great attraction for visitors to Glasgow thanks to its size and elegance. But despite his enormous fortune Robert Dreghorn had a bad reputation and was known as 'Bob Dragon', partly because of his pockmarked face – the result of an attack of smallpox at a time when there was no medical cure – and partly because he was reputed to be involved with dark forces. He was a woman fancier, but though he was well off and lived in considerable style he could never attract a girlfriend. Eventually, the lonely bachelor committed suicide and, for years after, sightings of his ghost, easily recognisable, were reported, usually following a woman as she walked home on her own. This, however, like the ghost of Cowden Mansion, is another instance in which the phantom simply disappeared. But the mansion in Great Clyde Street, which lay empty for years after Dreghorn's suicide, was at the centre of another incredible event. After a time George Provand, a wealthy paint merchant, took it on but became the unfortunate victim of the products he sold. It was at the time the resurrectionist scare was at its height and, early one morning, a group of revellers looked through the windows of the house and noticed red paint on the floor. Thinking it was blood, and that the

Provand family was engaged in the gruesome trade of bodysnatching, they broke in and wrecked the house, forcing George Provand to flee for his life. The guilty men were caught and severely punished, in accordance with the harsh standards prevalent in the early nineteenth century: the leader, Richard Campbell, was publicly scourged through the streets of the city (the last man to be so treated in Glasgow) and he and four others were transported to the colonies for fourteen years.

Many people have experience of apparitions. In most cases, as with Bob Hambleton, these are one-off events, but some people experience multiple sightings or attract entities from the world beyond. In 1982, Bill Mutch – the security guard involved in the transport-museum haunting – had his first experience of ghosts when he worked at Pollok House. The incident happened around quarter to eight in the morning as Bill was opening the offices on the top floor of the building. As he walked past the curator's office he saw 'a young woman in a Victorian dress standing beside a chair'. A moment later she was gone. It turned out that the area had once been a nursery so it may be that the woman had a connection with the building, perhaps a nanny who had once looked after the children.

Bill Mutch also took a keen interest in events that occurred at the Kelvingrove art gallery and museum – situated just across the road from the transport museum – which has been the scene of many odd incidents. According to Bill, 'Most staff members have heard footsteps on the stone stairwell, followed by a big jump onto the main landing. One morning a worker went into the old tearoom and was confronted by the ghost of an old woman sitting there.'

It is also said that spirits can be disturbed when a building is refurbished. They become attached to an area, and, like the living, the dead can be affected by changes to their accustomed surroundings. The Kelvingrove museum underwent an extensive redevelopment, which lasted three years and cost almost £30 million. It's a test case as to whether the ghosts associated with the building will continue to haunt it and even whether the level of activity will increase. In the summer of 2006 I approached Bridget McConnell, the director of Glasgow museums, and asked permission to conduct a ghost survey of the museum and also to issue a questionnaire to staff about any experiences they may have had. I was delighted when Ms McConnell gave me the go ahead. In the interim I was contacted by psychic Peter Thomson who, as luck would have it, actually worked in the Kelvingrove and had an intimate knowledge of the layout and the ghosts linked to the building. In September 2006 I visited the museum and was accompanied on my investigation by Thomson. He acted as my guide and at the same time used his psychic abilities to contact any spirits present in the museum. I was interested, among other things, in determining whether there was a link between the strange energy force detected by dowsers, usually called ley lines, and the appearance of those entities we label ghosts. To detect ley energy it is necessary to use dowsing rods, which can be either made of wood or metal and are held one in each hand. The rods come together if the energy is present. I have used this technique in investigations at schools, castles and domestic apartments to detect strange presences, whether of phantoms or the energy fields that can cause illness. This was the first time I had dowsed in a museum and I was amazed at how quickly the rods reacted. There was a strong response at the first spot I chose, at the stairs leading to the upper floor, and all the way round the stairwell. This appeared to link in with the regular reports of ghostly footsteps at this spot.

I quickly realised that the pull was especially strong around certain exhibits. Psychics often say that they are in contact with one particular spirit from the 'other side', an entity that has particular knowledge of spiritual matters and acts as a guide filtering contact with the spirit world. The spirits of Native Americans, the 'Indians' who occupied the land that became the USA, are said to be particularly spiritual, as their way of life was so in tune with nature. Perhaps it should have come as no surprise, therefore, to discover that around the exhibits labelled 'Native American' the pressure on the dowsing rods was so strong that it almost knocked them out of my hands. It had a definite physical effect on the body, making my flesh vibrate; at the same time it felt as if my mind was being taken over. I compared it with other exhibits in close proximity, such as the collection of native masks from around the world. The rods responded, but the reaction was nothing like as strong as that experienced at the Native American section. Even though the Native American exhibits are thousands of miles from home could they be linking to some other-dimensional force? The spirits of their long-dead owners? It does open a whole new perspective on the decision taken in 1998 to return the famous Native American ghost shirt to descendants of the Sioux tribe in the USA. Peter didn't have the same feeling around this section, but I guessed that it could be because we were connecting at different levels or maybe holding the dowsing rods channelled in a strange effect.

A number of encounters with a spectre – that of a woman, the grey lady – had been reported in the east turret. I visited the turret with Peter, who sensed that the spirit of a lady was there with us. She was particularly linked to a small, now disused, area that was once a staff room. Whenever staff were in the room they had the feeling that someone was standing behind them, but when they turned to look there was no one there. Peter could see her in a frilly, cream dress, which looked as if it had been worn in the late 1800s. It had a V pattern at the neck, but this was covered with other fabric. She had salt-and-pepper hair tied up in a bun. He sensed that she normally wore glasses, but was not wearing them when he saw her. Peter felt he wanted to call her 'lady' and give her some kind of stature. Could this be the spirit of an important person in Glasgow society who was once connected to the museum?

In a long room used as offices, leading off from the turret, staff felt that the furniture had been moved occasionally, though the ghost in the turret did not seem to appear here. This is in keeping with most haunts, where the spectre responsible focuses on one location and rarely moves from it. This office connected the east turret, where we had just been, to the west turret on the opposite side. Although no sightings had been reported in this area, I had a strong reaction on the rods as I stepped out of the connecting office into the west turret. It reduced dramatically the further I moved away from the door. Peter used his pendulum and asked if a spirit was present. The response was negative, but Peter also asked if the woman from the east turret's husband was there and it replied 'yes'. It gave the name James.

On the first floor, opposite a painting of Queen Victoria opening the museum, Peter experienced chest pains, dizziness and a headache. He sensed the presence of a man and had difficulty in speaking. He also felt that his left eye was screwed up, which could have been a monocle that the spirit wore when alive. The spirit was standing, with one arm over the other, and had a pipe in his hand. Although it wasn't Abraham Lincoln – who, incidentally, was famously involved with spiritualism – he looked like him being tall and thin, with jet-black hair. There was something strange about the suit he was wearing, which was the colour of oatmeal. Peter was given the date January 1927 and thought the spirit might be visiting the gallery as he was looking at the Queen Victoria painting. Peter remarked that he sensed many spirit people and suggested that they might be touring the gallery as they had done when they were alive.

It was interesting to note those areas where Peter as a psychic and I, as a dowser, experienced similar reactions. We both felt a strong response at the *Christ of St John of the Cross* painting of 1951, by the surrealist artist Salvador Dali. Similarly, in the armoury, an extensive display of military exhibits brought a particularly strong reaction round the exhibit labelled 'mercenary', which has what can only be described as a sinister black visor. Peter sensed anger and a 'don't care anymore' feeling. The most powerful response occurred at the display called 'fateful story', which, in fact, was a section taken from a painting and then enlarged. There was an incredibly strong reaction at this spot as if a wall of energy was forcing the rods back.

It is interesting to note that a woman driving past the Kelvingrove saw a figure dressed in black on the roof above the staff entrance. When she looked again it had disappeared. There's a story that a suicide victim had taken his life at this spot. However, a dark figure, if not human, can represent many things. It could be the phantom of someone connected to the area or some other entity from realms beyond. Without evidence from similar sightings we can't be sure. I did learn though that people were instinctively drawn towards a door in the east turret, which led out on to the roof and it may be that this has some connection with the appearance and disappearance of the apparition the lady saw.

My overall impression, however, is that the museum is a location in which energy is being generated of the type that allows spirits to come through. The appearance of ghosts, however, can never be predicted and often requires a trigger of some kind. My guess is that we will have more reported sightings in the future.

The unpredictability of the phenomenon was demonstrated when, in 2006, for no apparent reason, a phantom invaded the corridors of the former BBC headquarters in Queen Margaret Drive, in the fashionable West End of the city. The ghost, a woman, wore an old-fashioned dress with long sleeves and a stiff, white collar. Her hair was tied back in a bun. She was seen by several people, some at close quarters. It was said that the ghost was linked to the history of the building, at one time a training school for nurses, which meant that corpses might have been stored on the premises. But why this should generate a haunting over a hundred years later is just another part of the puzzle.

Some types of ghosts seem constantly to reappear. It may well be asked: why so many green ladies? They can be found at a host of sites. Take Breeze castle. A relic of a bygone age, Breeze castle (or more correctly Balgray tower, built in 1820 by Captain Breeze, a tea baron) originally sat in splendid isolation in the countryside surrounding the city. Nearly two hundred years later it still survives, located now in the heart of Springburn, once an economic power-house but today an area characterised by post-industrial neglect. To call it a castle may be an exaggeration, but, however you describe it, the building boasts its own ghost. A green lady is said to walk up the fifty-step spiral staircase, which is the most notable feature of the house. Exactly who this spectre is remains unclear. Green is, of course, the traditional colour of fairies or mystic entities like Herne the Hunter, who is more popularly known as Robin Hood. Robin, although these days linked to England and especially Sherwood Forest, was in past times as closely identified with Scotland. Dressed in green, Robin was clearly an entity from another world. Psychics say that the green aura surrounding ghosts is a result of the processes that allows spirits or other entities to carry over into our world. Hence the many green ladies who appear in different locations from the Citizens theatre to Breeze castle and beyond.

However, there are also grey ladies and white ladies. Glasgow University's Pearce Lodge dates from the earliest years of the institution and is said to be haunted by a grey lady. In February 1989 a lady dressed in an old-fashioned grey hat and coat with a 'shiny' face walked up to the lodge entrance. The porter, anticipating the ringing of the door bell, undid the lock, but when he looked outside was astonished to find no one there. This, it seems, is the typical experience of those who have encountered this phantom.

It is interesting that in this case the grey lady is so called because she appears in grey-coloured clothing and not because of her aura. It is noticeable too that the apparition looks solid. The white lady of Annfield house seems to have been so called because of her pale appearance. But again, this may be due more to the aura linked to her materialisation than her actual physical appearance.

Most sightings tend to be of single phantoms. Sightings of multiple ghosts are rare. The Botanic Gardens is said to be the haunt of several ghosts and strange light phenomena. But the site of the Battle of Langside is reputedly haunted by hundreds of the soldiers who died at this key encounter, which took place in May 1568. The army of phantoms, tradition has it, only appear on the anniversary of the battle: 13 May. As recently as 1993, as midnight on 12 May arrived, a passer-by witnessed a mist rolling from the pond in Queen's Park on the site of the battle and within the mist it was possible to make out the forms of soldiers. Similar scenes have been witnessed by people in the area. Visions of wounded and bloodied troops have also been reported. However, there is no guarantee that the phantom soldiers will appear on cue, as those who have gathered expectantly on the eve of the anniversary will vouch. Ghosts don't materialise when we expect them to. This is a key problem, which makes it difficult for scientists as a group to accept the evidence for ghosts, however real the individual experience. But who can doubt that encounters with the dead will continue no matter what sceptics may say, just as they have done for millennia. A recurring bridge to the supernatural that links the people of today with our ancestors from the distant past.

# 4

# Poltergeists

It is said that the poltergeist, whose noisy presence has affected many a Glasgow household, needs intense bursts of energy in order to become active. But are we really dealing with a force generated by the spirits of the dead? And can the experience of those whose homes have been invaded by the poltergeist shed any light on this disturbing phenomenon? James Montgomery, whom I interviewed in his apartment near Dennistoun, has no axe to grind.[1] Incidents over which he has no control have just happened to him, some particularly frightening. And in spite of it all James has managed to keep a cool head and not jump to conclusions. I found his account all the more convincing for that. In September 1992 James had moved into a small flat in the East End. He soon began to feel that there was something odd about the place. In particular, the bedroom was much colder than the rest of the house, although there was no obvious reason why this should be the case. James, however, soon began to sense a presence in the flat though he was not, at first, alarmed by the feeling. But, after he had lived there for about eighteen months, odd things began to happen. Money he had left in the kitchen, amounting to almost £57, mysteriously disappeared. One evening his bedroom filled with what seemed like smoke. The smoke was quite thick, more perhaps like a heavy fog. It seemed to completely fill the room. But whenever James moved towards the bedroom, the smoke slowly disappeared only to appear again a few weeks later. He noticed unexplained smells, especially that of flowers, when, in fact, there weren't any in the flat. The noise of someone washing dishes could be heard in the kitchen, though as James lived alone there was clearly no one else there. On one occasion a photograph standing on top of the television shot off to land several feet away. An event witnessed by a neighbour. On another occasion a friend who placed a newspaper on the coffee table watched in amazement as it began to move and dropped over the side to the floor.

The bathroom was also a focus of activity. James found a dash of shaving foam on the bathroom mirror, which he knew shouldn't have been there just after he had discovered that the grill on his cooker had been switched on. While James shaved in the bathroom the door suddenly burst open. He recalled: 'I had just started shaving when the toilet door was kicked in. I went into the hall and my girlfriend said she had seen a dark shadow coming down the hall and it went right through the door.' According to James, Jane, a friend, heard repeated banging on the door when she was in the bathroom. She also saw an apparition of a tall person dressed in shrouds, which appeared through one wall and then disappeared through another. On another occasion, Jane found a small pendant that looked like a representation of the Virgin Mary hidden beneath a bowl. There was no explanation as to how it had got there, as James had not brought it to his flat. Among psychics these objects are known as apports: items that appear out of nowhere, possibly from another dimension.

Astonishingly, James seemed to have evidence that there was a 'presence' in his home. A photograph taken of him standing in front of a doorway inside the flat shows a shadowy, human-shaped figure behind him. The figure looks solid, like a person, and analysis has shown it is neither a double exposure nor a technical disturbance on the negative. The figure is slightly taller than James and appears to be wearing a jacket.

The figure caught by the camera may explain another incident. James came home one day and saw a silhouette of a person sitting in his favourite living-room chair. He was so shocked that he immediately left the room and sat up all night with the light on. He only felt confident enough to return to the room the following morning and was relieved to find the chair empty. James described what life was like in the flat at this time: 'I would lie in bed and clearly hear the sound of dishes being washed. It was as if "someone" had been in the kitchen, but I knew there just couldn't be.' All sorts of strange things used to happen. Whenever James put up new wallpaper it would lose its colour and turn grey. James added: 'I had a hatch in the living room. One day I came back and found a light bulb lying on the hatch. It had been taken out of the bedroom somehow and been left there. I've no idea how it got there.' Electrical apparatus repeatedly broke down, including several television sets, vacuum cleaners and refrigerators. Light bulbs continually flickered, but electricians could find no fault with the supply. On another occasion, when James had left the flat and drove past on the bus, he noticed that the jardinière curtains had been lifted up and tucked in, though he had let them down.

James, however, unlike many who find themselves sucked into the world of the poltergeist, does not have a history of psychic experiences stretching back into childhood. The first strange incident he recalls occurred in 1971, when he was already an adult, in a house in Dennistoun when 'something like tar appeared and spread over the ceiling and walls. The kitchen taps turned on by themselves.' It certainly seems as if James is acting like some kind of catalyst, a channel to another world. The phenomena were not confined to one location and appeared to follow him from place to place. In his most recent flat James has experienced a continuation of the phenomena, particularly in their effect on electrical equipment. Room lights flash on and off. He was talking about a friend who had died and a light bulb shot out of a lamp and bounced across the carpet. Was this a poltergeist or the effect of some strange energy coming from James himself? A time switch started turning all by itself so that lights in the flat kept coming on at the wrong time. On another occasion James told me: 'I heard someone shouting my name.' Then, in July 2005, both James and his home help saw a shadow move silently down the hall. He has also observed golden orbs moving around his home, a phenomenon generally accepted by psychics as a sign of a spirit presence. But what kind of spirit? Friend or foe? Good or bad? James left a blank cassette tape running to test if any spirit activity might be recorded. When he played back the tape he heard a string of vulgar words coupled with the sounds of something growling. James decided against repeating the experiment. And who can blame him?

But do the activities of the poltergeist adequately explain the bizarre series of events that occurred in a flat near the city centre almost thirty years ago? In the 1970s, Kenneth (who later wrote an account of the incident) lived with his wife in a second-floor tenement flat in Partick. The flat was small, with just a living room, bedroom and bathroom. The only source of heating was a gas fire located in the living room and it was here that the couple slept, in a bed recess as, in winter, this was the warmest part of the house. A February morning was to remain in Kenneth's memory for a long time. His wife woke up first. She couldn't believe the sight that confronted her and shook Kenneth awake. She was convinced that the flat had been broken into while they had been sleeping and told Kenneth that this is what had happened. Every pane of glass in the living-room window was shattered. The television set had been moved and now stood in the opposite corner of the room from where it normally sat. The sideboard had been knocked forward and would have fallen to the floor if it had not come to rest against the settee. It had been emptied of its contents, which lay scattered across the carpet. It looked like the gang from the movie *Clockwork Orange* had targeted the flat. But a quick investigation by Kenneth soon proved that in spite of their first impressions they had not, in fact, been the subject of a weird burglary. It was much stranger than that.

For a start, though the glass panes in the window had been broken, the frame was intact and so a thief could not have entered this way even if he had managed to climb two flights up the outside wall. That left the door as the entry point, but, when Kenneth examined it, it was still locked with the chain and bolt in place.

This was perplexing. But the proof that a really strange event had occurred while the couple slept could be seen in the bizarre change that had taken place in a number of objects. Every cup and saucer, every plate and bowl and tumbler, had been turned into fine sand. On the mantelpiece had stood a collection of brightly coloured ornaments; in their place now rested separate piles of multi-coloured sand, each small mound with its particular colour clear evidence of where an ornament had at one time been. An almost identical change had taken place in a collection of blue-and-white-striped bowls that had been transformed into blue-and-white piles of sand. And the most inexplicable part was that the battering the flat had received had taken place without waking either Kenneth or his wife. It had either been a completely soundless incident or, alternatively, something had kept the couple sleeping through this very odd event. But how on earth could that have happened?

Animals can be particularly sensitive to supernatural phenomena and having left the flat, Kenneth, as he describes in his article, returned with his father's Alsatian, although it is not clear whether it was intended for protection or to ascertain if the dog could sense a strange presence. When they reached the tenement block the dog refused to go inside. It was clearly upset and wouldn't enter the main hall, let alone go up to the flat itself. When Kenneth tried to pull him in the dog began to panic and started growling. Something was quite clearly disturbing the animal. Kenneth decided it was pointless trying to make it go any further and left. A few days later, however, Kenneth was forced to return to collect his belongings as the couple had decided not to stay in the flat. The room was as he had left it though he noticed the sand had gone and assumed it had been blown away. Although Kenneth didn't remark on it, that disappearance seems odd in itself. Had it vanished into another dimension or, indeed, simply been swept about the room by a draught of wind?

There were a number of contradictory effects that heighten the enigmatic nature of the event. Although the glass panes in the window had been broken no damage had been done either to the glass screen of the television or a glass door on the cooker. And although every pane in the window had been broken in what seemed to be an identical fashion there were still intact shards protruding from the frame. A mirror in the room had been cracked, but not shattered. It was if a force had cut through the window glass then shattered crockery and ground ornaments to fine dust while moving selected objects round the room. But how, and why? The couple's experience was no doubt an extreme example, but, at the same time, it is the typical activity of the poltergeist: a strange and powerful effect on physical surroundings, but with no obvious source for the disturbance.

But can we detect that source and, at the same time, solve another puzzle? Is there a connection between the spirits of the dead communicated with by psychics and the disruptive poltergeist? The entity seen by Jean Fraser in her Castlemilk flat may give a hint of what we are dealing with: a phenomenon neither phantom nor living being, but with the unnerving characteristics of both. In the 1980s Jean was heading from the kitchen to her bedroom and had to pass the living room on the way. The door was slightly ajar and when Jean glanced in she thought she saw someone sitting on the couch. Taken aback, Jean decided to go no further than the doorway and cautiously flicked the light on. Now in the full glare of the light she could clearly see the figure of an elderly woman, one who looked like a 'real' person. She had her arms and legs crossed and was looking over at the window. Her white hair reached to her shoulders and she was wearing a woolly cardigan with a skirt reaching just above her ankles. Unlike the traditional ghost the figure looked solid. It seemed almost alive till it began to fade away, then it just disappeared. Later, a neighbour confided to Jean that the description matched that of a woman who had died in the house, some years before Jean had moved in. Spirits, psychics tell us, can become attached to their home, resent intruders and not want to leave, but the being encountered here had a more substantial form than the traditional ghostly apparition. It suggests a different type of phantom. And one you would not have been surprised to see stand up and touch or move objects in the room where it had been sitting. Is the poltergeist 'simply' a spirit that can somehow assume a solid form? Although that would appear a likely scenario the evidence is that these noisy spirits usually prefer the cloak of invisibility as opposed to putting in an appearance.

The truth is that ghosts appearing in the home can, by their very nature, appear more disturbing than those encountered in other locations. It can seem like an invasion of your personal space. And often those spectres that appear seem to wish to make their presence felt to an extent that can appear obsessional. Somehow these spirits seem able to interact with their surroundings, especially with people, and the phantoms involved can appear solid and alive. A poltergeist can certainly come across as one of the most frightening of all the supernatural phenomena an individual might encounter. As far back as the 1670s, in Keppoch, an invisible force threw stones and set a house on fire. Referred to as a devil at the time, today we would see it as classic poltergeist phenomena. No doubt many similar incidents have been forgotten over the years, but recently there appears to have been an increase in poltergeist activity. Bizarre encounters with strange beings that make you wonder if we really are simply dealing with spirits of the dead, as many psychics would have us believe. Or, as those interested in the occult would argue, have we brushed against some other world or dimension filled with living entities whose own reality is completely different from our own?

Poltergeist phenomena seem to strike without any rhyme or reason. In the early hours of 23 June 2004 Janice Gray from Johnstone was disturbed when, without warning, two very large eyes, almond-shaped and amber-coloured, appeared in a room in her flat.[2] They just seemed to be floating in the dark watching her. Janice didn't catch sight of an entity, and the lights were off, but she judged that whatever the eyes belonged to could not be very large. She was seated at the time and the weird eyes were at the level of her head, just a few feet away. Eventually, they simply faded away. Around the same period Janice was watching a film when suddenly a high-pitched sound erupted from the television set. It carried on for a while and had an unnerving resonance. Janice felt sure that the neighbours would complain, but the vibration stopped as suddenly as it had started. Just as strange was the unexpected disappearance one day of a gold ring which Janice always wore. A thorough search was made, but it seemed to have gone for good. The only place left to look was the rubbish bin, but just as she was going to search it the ring appeared out of nowhere, back on her hand. It was an incident witnessed by Janice's partner. All of these incidents added together seem like the typically pointless activities associated with a poltergeist. But if a spirit was involved, what was it up to?

Paul Anderson's experience brings together solid entities and inexplicable phenomena and though giving a clearer insight into the nature of the poltergeist leaves both puzzles and clues.[3] In the 1960s Paul lived on the fourth floor of a tenement at Govan Cross. He told me:

> One night I awoke and there was a man kneeling at the foot of the bed. I sat up and looked at him and asked: 'What are you doing here?' He lifted his right arm and pointed upwards. I looked up and gradually a light appeared. It became brighter and then I saw the figure of a person with their arms outstretched. He was horizontal, floating about a foot below the ceiling. I have never seen anything so bright. Then the light disappeared and the man was gone. I thought he looked like a priest or a monk and about forty years old. Good looking and clean shaven. He had short, thin, black hair brushed back. He wore a brown, or dark, coat of heavy material that buttoned up to his chin. Not floppy like a habit but neatly tailored. I was of the opinion

that other people were standing behind him. I was terrified for months, then I told my wife and friends.

This encounter disturbed Paul for twenty years and in the 1980s he was told by a monk that someone of his calling would not wear the type of habit he had described seeing. So if it was not a monk what was it? Paul learned that 'Druids once worshipped in the Govan Cross area'. However, given Paul's description it is unlikely that the 'spirit' he saw was a Druid. It's not the sort of clothing that a man from the time of the Druids would wear. So what could it have been? Although to Paul it had religious overtones, particularly with the intense light often associated with a religious encounter and the outstretched arms like Jesus on the cross, the incident might not have any connection to a biblical revelation. It's noticeable that Paul felt 'disturbed' by the experience more than exalted. Perhaps there was a message for Paul, but it could also have been one of those inexplicable events in which, for no apparent reason, the veil between this world and the next suddenly opens. More events followed, some persistent and repetitive, suggesting that Paul or something within the building was acting as the trigger.

Out of the blue one night, while Paul and his wife were sitting in the living room, they heard the sounds of a young baby crying. It was coming from the bedroom. Paul recalled: 'But when I opened the door the crying stopped. This went off and on for years. I checked time and again with the neighbours, but no baby was found or was visiting.' When Paul eventually left the house in the 1970s he took out the bedroom fireplace, suspecting that he would discover the skeleton of a child. He could be forgiven for thinking that a disturbed spirit was the cause of the crying, but there was nothing there. It is interesting to note that, traditionally, the sound of a crying baby is a tactic used by poltergeists to disturb a household. It's a sound that most adults are unable to ignore. So was the crying baby some spirit trick just to torment the Andersons?

That the events in the house were linked to poltergeist activity is confirmed by an incident that you would only expect to experience in a horror film. Paul recalled:

> One Friday at 5.30 p.m. my wife and I were standing talking in the living room. On the wall was a cardboard calendar held by a nail. Around the nail holding the calendar hung a broken chain with a crucifix suspended from it. The chain and cross started to swing to and fro hitting against the calendar. Then it began to spin round and round, faster and faster. As suddenly as it started, it stopped. My wife and I were left holding each other in fright.

Was there some presence in the house that resented the sign of the cross? Or was some other message intended?

Poltergeist activity has a long pedigree and some events are of such intensity that they imprint themselves on the memory of successive generations. One such incident from the early years of the twentieth century – and first recorded by the eminent ghost-hunter, Elliott O'Donnell[4] – involves a house bordering Blythswood Square. The man who bought the property, William, sensed it had a disturbed atmosphere, but his wife loved the place. The decor and fittings were past their sell-by date, especially the bathroom. That was immediately revamped and a new bath put in. William's sense of unease in the house did not go away. He felt especially uncomfortable in the bathroom, so tended to leave the door slightly ajar whenever possible. One day William slipped and fell in the bathroom, the light went out and he found himself in the dark. It was one of those rare occasions when he had locked the door behind him. As he picked himself up, and fumbled for the door handle, he heard the sound of someone splashing in the bathtub. He was then aware of a door creaking open and a female form appeared through what once must have been an entry into the bathroom, but which had long been walled over and hidden behind a cupboard. There was a strange, phosphorescent glow around her, and, ignoring William, she walked directly towards the bath. From the choking sounds which followed William was convinced that the woman had murdered the person sitting in the tub. It had been a terrifying experience, but he did not want to upset his wife and children so he kept quiet about the event. A few days later, however, as his son was running a bath, the swollen body of an old man suddenly appeared beneath the water. The son ran out of the room, but when the rest of the family arrived to investigate the bath was empty. However, minutes later they caught sight of a young, attractive and well-dressed woman who walked down the stairs then disappeared straight through a boarded-up door. It emerged that, according to local gossip, an older husband had been murdered in the house by his young bride anxious to get hold of his money and marry a younger lover. Whether or not this explains the events in the house it is clear that something odd was going on. We don't just have phantoms, but figures that can apparently use solid objects. Spectres that open doors and splash water around. Dead people with flesh-and-blood bodies.

Move forward a hundred years and round the corner to Blythswood Street. Number 123 stands where Blythswood Street and Blythswood Square meet. It is an old building used these days as offices and, in the basement, there is a recording studio.[5] Originally, however, it had been a house for the city's wealthier inhabitants and then converted into luxury flats. In the 1990s it was badly gutted by fire, which as well as destroying a good part of the property and resulting in complete refurbishment, also had an unexpected effect. It seemed to end the activities of the poltergeist that had haunted the site for years. In this case it does seem to have been the classic 'noisy spirit' that the word poltergeist means. People who worked in the basement, used by the BBC, reported hearing sounds of people walking around on the floor overhead. When they went to investigate they found the rooms locked and it was clear that no one could have got in. The rooms were, in fact, quite deserted.

In the basement the noise of people banging doors was often

heard at night by employees working on their own. Because of the nature of the work people could often be by themselves late on. They were well aware that they were alone in the building and so could quickly pick up any unexplained noise or movement. Witnesses also reported hearing voices in the basement area, raised voices as if people were engaged in a shouting match. And, as is often the case in events of this nature, people sensed a 'presence', as if someone was standing close behind them. But when they turned to look there was no one there. It was unnerving. People felt so uncomfortable about the atmosphere in the building that some staff refused to work on their own at night. Some expressed the opinion that before the fire the feeling in the building had been quite simply 'horrible'.

Where a poltergeist is involved there is usually a focus for events and the general view was that in number 123 this area was the camera-and-tape store, which had a particularly disturbing atmosphere. One explanation for the events was that a woman had either hung herself in the building or had been murdered, probably strangled, with a rope. There is no direct evidence for this, but there is always the possibility that at the root of events of this type there lies a distressed spirit. It is interesting to note that the workmen involved in refurbishing the building and who had worked on it previously, reported hearing the same phenomena. Number 123 at one time seems to have had a corridor that linked directly to a house in Blythswood Square. Although it may be significant, it's more likely that the explanation for two buildings situated so closely together being affected by poltergeist activity lies in the energy lines that are running through the area. It is this unexplained force, called ley lines by dowsers, which seems to facil-itate the appearance of ghosts and poltergeists. This may explain why the storeroom at 123 seemed such a focus. The energy would pass through the building at a specific location and, having created a kind of focal vortex, poltergeist activity would spread out from here like ripples on the surface of a loch. So why did the disturbance stop with the fire? There seems no obvious connection. It could simply be coincidence although using fire to destroy demons and other strange entities like vampires is a well-established tradition.

It may be significant to note that phantoms of humans are not the only ghosts seen. A house in Duke Street was once rented by a family whose children started to play with something that had the appearance of a furry dog. The family didn't own a pet and the creature seemed to turn up in the stair and wander into the flat at any time of the day. It didn't seem to belong to anyone and appeared friendly enough. However, there was one odd thing that the children noticed. They could never quite touch the dog. Somehow it was always just out of reach. The family eventually moved out, but soon others were reporting sightings of the strange beast. An investigator who went to see for himself witnessed a large dog disappearing into a wall halfway up the stairs. So, as some psychics claim, the spirits of animals maybe do live on. In fact sightings of phantom dogs, usually black, are reported from various parts of the country. It is noticeable that the animal ghost of Duke Street was able to interact with its surroundings. Just like the typical poltergeist. But, it might be asked, why only dogs? Are there no phantom cats or birds or other types of animals? The answer might be that there are, but we just don't notice them. It is also possible that if ghosts are, as some suggest, printed on the building because of an acute emotional incident that animals are just not affected in the same way. Of course, according to some this might not be the spectre of a dead animal, but one that has wandered in from another dimension. The phantom dog, however, in spite of its poltergeist traits did not seem to be on a mission to upset the occupants of the house. Far from it. In that sense it was markedly different from the human variety.

In other cases the effect of a poltergeist on an individual can be disturbing, but sometimes its presence can have strange repercussions. In the 1970s an incident took place that was so bizarre the police became involved. On 3 November 1974 Mr and Mrs

Bill Thomson[6], who lived in the Balornock district of the city, were disturbed by strange noises that seemed to be coming through the floor of their home. They assumed the source was the flat below, which was occupied by another couple, Mr and Mrs Grant Smith. They too had heard strange sounds but to them they appeared to be coming through the ceiling from their neighbours upstairs. The sounds were quite distinct: a repeated banging and scraping, loud enough to be heard above voices on the television. It was so intrusive that eventually the police were called as residents were convinced that somebody in the building was deliberately causing a disturbance. A charge emphatically denied by the two families at the centre of the activity. But, in spite of a police presence, the noise continued for the following two nights. Eventually, Mr and Mrs Smith left the flat to stay with relatives. During the time they were away not only did the noises continue, but also a range of poltergeist phenomena were observed. According to Mr and Mrs Thomson, who had decided to stay in their flat, ornaments and furniture moved of their own accord. Clock hands spun round the dial. Musical tunes were tapped out on different objects throughout the house. In spite of investigation by the police, housing officials and building experts, no obvious source could be found to explain the disturbance. Psychics who visited expressed the view that the building was definitely haunted. A professor from Glasgow University who investigated the event confirmed that there was something odd going on, though he believed it could be to do with 'psychic energy'. This is a force that anyone can radiate, but some radiate it more strongly than others and it can have a wide impact. Even the police were forced to admit that, 'there is something strange in that house. Something we cannot logically explain.' The Thomson family had come to the same conclusion and Bill admitted: 'Now my family is too afraid to sleep in the bedroom and we have asked the corporation for a transfer.'

The incidents at Balornock were short lived and confined to one area. But what happens when a poltergeist infestation lasts for years and follows a person whether he is at work, at home or sitting with friends in a pub? I first met John Adams at his Drumchapel flat when I was researching material for my 'X-Files' column in the *Evening Times*.[7] I have had several discussions with him since. John, now in his early sixties, is Glasgow born and bred. He left school, Balshagray annex, at fifteen and held down a variety of jobs that included working in the shipyards at Elderslie and a spell in the army. He struck me at our first meeting, and I have never changed my view, as a level-headed individual who told of his strange experiences in a calm manner that gave no outward hint of the disturbing events that he had been forced to endure. In John's case the entity that attached itself to him did not initially make its presence felt in his house, but in the workplace. Thereafter, it only gradually drew closer to him and began to disrupt his home life. John found himself involved in a never-ending struggle to get rid of the strange being from another world. It was quite simply a series of events that must go down in the history of psychic phenomena as the longest and most intense ever recorded.

John's experiences started in the 1970s when he was working with a contractor on a gas-storage station in Kilmarnock. The first sign that something odd was taking place occurred when stones started flying through the air, bouncing off the tank and bothy hut as if deliberately aimed. They came out of nowhere and there was never any sign of who might have thrown them. It was strange, but everyone shrugged their shoulders and carried on with the job. Next, the keys to the gas-station gate kept disappearing, to be discovered hidden in cracks in the wall surrounding the site. This happened several times, and although there was a suspicion that someone was having a daft joke it happened so many times that it would have been impossible for the worker responsible for the hoax not to have been spotted. Only a few men were employed there and the site covered a small area. People couldn't avoid keeping an eye on each other. Nerves were now beginning to fray. But more shocks were in store. All kinds of objects started disappearing only to reappear in unlikely places. One day when one of the gas-board managers appeared he was 'greeted' with a hail of bricks, thrown by an invisible hand, which battered against the roof and bonnet of his car as he was getting out. The reason for this bizarre assault was to emerge later.

John and his team moved to Lanark to work at another gas station, hoping that they had left the strange incidents behind. But whatever had appeared at Kilmarnock followed them. Stones from nowhere hitting the side of the storage tank were the first sign. But, then, whatever was behind the disturbance started to commun-icate. A metal platform circled the tank and the men would walk round it while they were chatting. It didn't take long to do the walk, but as they did so the wall that was adjacent to the tank was out of sight for a short while. It was on this wall that strange messages started to appear. The first sign that something unearthly was happening was the appearance of the single letter 'R' scratched into the wall plaster. It looked roughly done as if it had been made by a stone. Then the word 'Rocky' appeared, with the word 'freend' below. 'Rocky' was John's nickname. It seemed obvious that the entity was trying to communicate directly with him. Disturbing though this clearly was, John wanted to learn more and started asking questions. He would scratch a question on the wall and in the time it took him to circle the tank and return to his starting point a reply would appear on the plaster. As John admits, 'it was a surreal experience'. They learned that the spirit they were dealing with had a name. It called itself 'Jonathon', but often signed with the initials 'JV'. They never found out what the 'V' stood for. The 'spirit' never explained.

From then on, wherever they went, the spirit or presence of Jonathon went with them. At their next work site in Motherwell the bothy door flew open and a pickaxe came shooting in, narrowly missing those inside. It seemed deliberately calculated to avoid hitting people, but to terrify them at the same time. One day a newspaper floated out of the sky and lodged in the fence. When

Harry, one of the workers, picked it up it had 'JV' on it. The initials of Jonathon.

Even bigger objects started to materialise. One day as they walked round the gantry they found their path blocked by a pile of wood. But by the time they returned to the same spot the wood had disappeared. Notes appeared from nowhere with a skull and crossbones. This, it turned out, was Jonathon's 'mark', although he wouldn't reveal why he used it. One day, John asked: 'Why did you follow us?' The reply scratched into the wall by the 'presence' was that it used to live there and the gas board had built over his home. The spirit continually asked for help, but never explained why it needed help or what help it required. An attempt was made by some of the workers to contact Jonathon using an Ouija board. John decided that he didn't want to have anything to do with this attempt to link with the spirit world, so he sat outside the bothy. A few minutes after the impromptu séance started he heard a bang and a milk bottle came crashing down from the sky. Inside the bothy a large chest of drawers started rocking to and fro of its own accord, repeatedly striking the side of the hut. The experiment was abandoned and never tried again.

Jonathon seemed reluctant to let John go and each day as they drove back to Glasgow from work those in the van could feel a force pulling the vehicle backwards. It was as if the poltergeist needed their presence at the storage tank. On one occasion a hard hat flew through the van and cut the driver across the face. Were they somehow, however unintentionally, facilitating the appearance of the poltergeist? Was Jonathon drawing his energy from their presence? Does this explain why he was so desperate not to lose contact with them?

Unfortunately for John it seems that Jonathon, whoever or whatever he really was, had followed him back to his house. One day the curtains started to flutter though there was no wind outside. Then they lifted till they were standing straight out from the curtain rail. Next the coffee table flipped over. One of the legs broke off and flew across the room to embed itself in the door. A cigarette shot out of his friend Bill's hand and splattered against the wall sending out a mass of sparks. When Bill went into the kitchen an iron flew off the sideboard and hit him in the face. It seemed like a deliberate attempt to injure him. But it wasn't all violence. Jonathon could do amazing things for no apparent reason. Twice in a matter of seconds he, or it, solved the Rubik's Cube puzzle. John simply put the cube, mixed up, behind his back and when he took it out, it was done with every side the same colour. There were several witnesses to this strange feat.

Even when socialising John could not escape the attentions of Jonathon. Nor could his friends and workmates. Sitting one day in the Exchequer pub in Partick, coins started flying through the air and bouncing-off tables. A piece of paper came shooting out of nowhere and when it was opened it read, 'Rocky help JV'. Then a waitress came over and said there was a call for Rocky. When John went to the phone there was no one on the line, but he could hear a strange background noise, like something from outer space. Thirty minutes later the same thing happened after he had once more been called to the phone. John asked a man who was sitting next to the phone if he had heard it ring but he said that he hadn't. But stranger events were to follow. Tom, John's friend, had a spot of lager left in a long glass. Out of nowhere a coin dropped out of the air and landed in the bottom of the glass. The lager started to foam up and filled the glass, spilling onto the table and then onto the floor. But the most bizarre incident of all was about to happen. Robert, another friend, went to the cigarette machine and having made his purchase sat back down. He unsealed the cigarette packet and, flipping over the lid, turned white. Immediately, he crumpled up the packet and threw away the cigarettes untouched. A message had been written inside the packet, but Robert refused to reveal what it said. Robert kept asking John: 'How did you do it?' He found the incident so shocking that he had convinced himself an exceptionally clever trick had been played on him. But as John said: 'How did he think we could interfere with a cigarette machine and put a marked cigarette packet inside it? It's not possible.' Robert never revealed what the message said, but John had no doubt that Jonathon had again made contact.

Evidence that within this varied poltergeist activity there may be, at bottom, one linking phenomenon can be seen in a truly odd incident. One reminiscent of events at the Partick flat involving Kenneth described earlier. When John came into his living room one morning a bottle of whisky had been ground into a pile of sand finer than dust. The label and the top, however, were still in one piece. What weird force could have been responsible for such an extraordinary event? One that seems to defy the laws of physics. Meanwhile other inexplicable incidents occurred, all so typical of a poltergeist infestation, in being, on the face of it, wholly meaning-less. Spaghetti strips fell on to the table and formed into the shape of a skull and crossbones, Jonathon's calling card, announcing his presence. Peas, falling from a kitchen worktop, formed themselves into a question mark on the floor. To John this was more fright-ening than anything because it was so ludicrous. It just didn't seem to make any sense. Notes appeared from nowhere with the single word 'why' written on them. A pirate ship that John guessed must have required thousands of matches to make, and would have taken hours of work, appeared overnight in his living room. It was like the destruction seen in Kenneth's Partick flat in reverse. A variety of similar objects appeared, all of which John destroyed. Under-standably, he was reluctant to keep objects of such a weird origin lying in his home for any length of time. One day John heard sledgehammer-type noises in the rafters of his house. The noise went on and on as if whoever or whatever was causing it was going mad. Then it stopped and so did Jonathon. 'It was the last I heard of him', said John. Did this disturbance indicate that, by whatever strange means, the 'other side' had been opened for Jonathon, and it was now closing? It seems more than a coincidence that this event marked the poltergeist's last contact.

But though Jonathon had left it was not the last time John was to feel the influence of the 'other side'. Around October 1995 John felt the presence of a poltergeist again. This one was even more determined than Jonathon. It attacked John every night while he lay in bed, throwing him around the room. John felt that he needed help and contacted a local psychic who 'put hands on him' to rid John of the spirit presence. John started shaking violently and felt as if something was coming out of him, but the process wasn't completed. Frustrated, John visited a local church where another psychic attempted to free him of the spirit presence. As hands were again laid on him John felt as if a 'demon' was being drawn from him, but as before he was convinced that the demon had not been fully expelled from his body. It made him more determined than ever to get rid of the presence in his flat. He thought he might be able to communicate with it and get a better understanding of what was going on. At first John used a pendulum, asking questions and getting answers as the weight, suspended on a cord, moved in response picking letters from the alphabet and gradually building up a sentence. However, John soon found that the 'spirit' could work directly through him. By using automatic writing, effectively allowing the 'presence' to control his arm, he soon had many messages; messages, however, that raised many more questions than answers. John knew that it was some other power that was guiding his hand because the writing was so different from his own. The messages always began 'we want you to do' such and such. Although John had longed to communicate he quickly found that it had a down side. It was as if, he admitted, he had 'tuned into hell'.

By contacting the poltergeist had he unwittingly encouraged its activity? It seemed to gather strength from the contact and began to take over. It would jerk John awake and then force him to write. It would signal its presence by thumping furniture in the bedroom and banging on the roof. Objects placed on the table by his bed would be thrown to the floor. Doors slammed for no reason. Furniture moved by itself. At night he felt his legs being pulled. It was as if a presence was hovering over him. Most frightening of all he had the feeling that an invisible entity was trying to enter his body. In John's case the spirit entities weren't just out to cause a nuisance. They were also giving messages: threats, gibberish, but also some fascinating claims.

Many of the messages John received were disturbing. One read: 'In December 1992 I got involved in a fight with (name deleted) in Drumchapel and he killed me. I am (name deleted) from Balornock and I'm being held in your body by demons.' Another message read, 'I will get out of your body now. You must believe that I'm going to leave you. And you must be brave as you will feel groggy and you will be sick.' And again, 'I will not be flesh much longer as I am getting weaker and I won't be getting any more power as you have found a believer who is praying for you. You are fading and I won't be able to possess you anymore after tonight.' John eventually received hundreds of messages from all kinds of spirits. It was as if he had linked up with a phone network in a spirit world. Many names of spirits and demons were given to him, as well as parts of messages that on their own did not make a great deal of sense. 'I am going in half an hour. I must leave your body before I go and you will have to go to bed before then. And you must take the crosses off and be brave.' One claimed to come from a world beyond our galaxy, indicating that it had top-secret information about a UFO crash in the Arizona desert in 1961. Several messages, in fact, claimed to come from entities from other planets. Is this evidence that the spirit and UFO phenomena are linked in some yet unclear way? Or is the mischievous poltergeist up to its well-worn tricks? John reported strange balls of light in his bedroom, signs that a door to another dimension had opened.

So why did John become such a target? One investigator told him: 'You invited them in' and he advised John to keep the radio and light on in his bedroom because it kept poltergeists away. John, an ex-army man, has done this ever since. Interestingly, although the events at Kilmarnock and their aftermath had appeared as if from nowhere, John had experienced a strange incident some years before. During his army days in Germany soldiers in their barracks were disturbed by strange noises coming from the attic. An investigation revealed nothing, but the men felt there was a strange atmosphere there, that indescribable feeling that occasionally grips us when we sense a 'presence'. Irrational maybe, but real nonetheless. It was a small incident, but one that made a big impression on John.

While John had reason to be afraid of the 'presence' he kept surprisingly calm even though he believes that in his previous house a poltergeist tried to kill him by pressing his face into a cushion. On another occasion he saw the shape of a creature about six-feet tall. But its form was made out by twisted strands of what appeared to be an electrical discharge, red and blue. John could see right through it. He recalled: 'I felt it walking towards me and getting inside me'. That was when he first started to feel that 'something' had actually taken his body over. John witnessed many strange sights. He even experienced a succubus, the phenomenon of spirits or demons inside the human body; he reported that he could feel them moving inside him. On another occasion he saw a creature which looked like an orang-utan, but with a human face. John believes there are seven demons in his house, but many more 'out there'. The pendulum gave the message, 'we are legion', and John believes them. He has seen them and experienced what they are capable of. He asks: 'With such incredible powers why don't they take over the world?' The answer is, John explains, 'they're being stopped by something'. On one occasion the 'presence' told John it would have to go because 'the white witch is here'. To John this is confirmation that though there are forces for evil there are equally powerful forces for good.

At one point John made a list of all the effects that the spirits had had on him. It reads: 'It's attacked me four times (once in church). It makes me very anxious and itchy. It's tried to suffocate me. It's made me do all sorts of things. It moves the lights, slams doors and moves carpets.' The spirits gave themselves odd names including Jinfer, a demon, Ceber, Volfufnah and Ruster. Nonsensical names on the face of it, but which echo the strange names used by demonologists through the centuries to describe demons under the control of Satan. Names supposedly dictated by these powerful entities themselves. Astaroth. Rosier. Leviathan. Three of many. Names that appear similar to those given by the spirit entities to John. One demon who said his name was Ibeza, and claimed to be an 'angel', told John, 'I am going to catch Jonathon for you,' John asked: 'Is it Jonathon torturing me?' Answer 'Yes'. John: 'But why? He said he was my friend.' To which the 'angel' replied, 'No he isn't. He was just pretending.' John Adams found communicating with the spirit confusing. In the end he tended to the view that the spirit was evil, 'it never tells the truth'. Maybe the poltergeist simply has no objective other than confusing its victims.

John's story is undoubtedly a strange one, but he insists that it all happened. Much of it is confirmed by events experienced by others subjected to poltergeist interference. Events in John's house seem like a confirmation of our worst nightmares. But as John believes, for all the disturbance that they cause, there seems an even more powerful force holding the poltergeist back.

We must hope he is right.

## Notes

[1] See also Dr Peter McCue's article in the October 2003 edition of *Paranormal Review*.

[2] Communication to author.

[3] Communication to author.

[4] Elliott O'Donnell, *Scottish Ghost Stories*, 1911

[5] Communication to author.

[6] See also *Glasgow Herald*, 17 January 1975. All names changed in this account.

[7] See Ron Halliday, 'Secret Meaning of the Spirit Messenger' *Evening Times*, 2 August 1997.

# 5

# Weird Stories

It is only to be expected that a city which emerged from a mystic past would attract some very bizarre events. Incidents that are impossible to explain or categorise. Glasgow has experienced more than its fair share. It would be wrong to say that nothing connects these events. They stand out as strange and inexplicable, challenging the reality that surrounds us. They raise questions as to what exactly is going on in the world. Are appearances deceptive?

At the entrance to the Crown Gardens housing development in the New Gorbals, where Malta Terrace meets Kidston Terrace, hangs a bronze sculpture, *The Gatekeeper*. Mystics claim the figure is as mysterious as similar phenomena that attract thousands to churches across the world. Is it Scotland's equivalent of the Turin shroud? Soon after the statue was first unveiled in 2002 a red liquid was seen flowing from the outstretched palm of its right hand. To believers it is blood, or at least symbolic blood, running from the point on the statue's hand where nails pinioned Christ's outstretched arms to the cross. The statue is, of course, that of an angel rather than of Jesus, but the religious significance of this bizarre phenomenon for those who believe in it is just as if it was Christ himself. The fact that the statue is made of bronze – which is particularly noted for its resistance to corrosion – suggests that the red liquid cannot be explained away by the cynics among us as a natural process. So is this a signal from another world, a sign that miracles can happen, even in our technology-driven world?

During the Christmas holidays, on the evening of 27 December 1992, William McRoberts was driving to the Paisley Megabowl along the A726, close to Glasgow airport. In the back were his wife and one-year-old son. In the front passenger seat sat his brother, Jim. William was aware that the car ahead was travelling unusually slowly. It then came to a sudden halt. In William's words:

> This puma came plodding along. It was full in the head-lights. I saw the whole face. It was about the size of an Alsatian, but more muscular. It was a definite fawn colour. I could see the flash of its eyes. It powered over the fence effortlessly. It was six-to-eight feet away from me when I saw it. It was very nonchalant.

The car in front of William then shot off. William reversed to the gates of the runway and managed to shine his headlights into a field. There was nothing there. But what amazed him even more was that no one else in his car had seen the beast.

He called the police and they arrived about twenty minutes later. It turned out the man in the car in front had seen the puma, and that other witnesses in Erskine had also reported sightings of the animal. However, their descriptions were of a black beast rather than the fawn colour William had seen, although that may have been due to William having had a close-up view. The following day he returned to the spot and although there was snow on the ground there were, unusually, no signs of any tracks. William's view was that:

> It must have come through the airport perimeter fence. It had a long, thick tail. I was only eight feet from its face and I could see the whole length of the animal. It leapt the fence at my car. It was between 7.30 and 8 p.m. It didn't look at the cars or appear to be disturbed at our presence.

He added that his brothers had come across sheep carcasses hanging on trees in Neilston Pad, which is a flat-top hill and the highest point in the area. So does this suggest that we are dealing with a flesh-and-blood beast? Or do the lack of tracks and the way the creature seemed unaware of the presence of the cars suggest that we are dealing with a phantom? In August 1976 a bizarre incident took place on a farm just outside Glasgow. Several geese were killed in identical fashion, the only marks on their body being puncture wounds the same depth and distance apart. A wire fence had been ripped open to get at the birds and the farm's Alsatian was discovered cowering in its den. The general view was that a puma was responsible and, in fact, reports of an animal that resembled one had been made in recent years. Lorry driver Hugh Gilmour almost ran over a big-cat lookalike that bounded across the road in front of him in the summer of 1974.

In fact, sightings of a puma-shaped creature have come in from a wide area round the city. Added to this evidence is the unexplained disappearance of a variety of domestic pets. This is not a recent phenomenon. In February 1911 a letter to the *Glasgow Herald*, headed 'Dog Stealing', complained: 'Can nothing be done by the police to prevent the cruel practice of dog stealing? One inquires for one's lost dog and receives the reply, "Oh it is likely despatched safely out of the country by this time." Can anyone give information about who despatches them?'

Fast forward to 1990. The unexplained disappearance of domestic animals had reached such a peak that people were warned to keep an eye on their pets by the authorities. Cats and small dogs seemed particularly at risk. But who could be behind such a strange phenomenon? There was some suggestion that animals were being taken for illegal fighting, but that is hardly a satisfactory explanation given the numbers. Thousands disappeared in one year alone. Could it be down to a predator? This, along with witchcraft and black magic, was one area of speculation given the reports of 'phantom pumas'. A big cat would certainly take a cat or dog or any smaller creature given the chance. Yet the kidnapped animals seemed to vanish completely, with no evidence, in the shape of bones or other remains, to explain their fate. Some have speculated that these creatures have been taken by alien entities or beings from other dimensions as specimens to examine. No one, however, has reported encountering such an abduction though there have been reports of alien abductees seeing animals on board the space-craft they claimed they have been taken to. It may stretch the bounds of credulity to imagine that beings from other worlds are capturing pets, but no more than the idea that humans are being abducted. Killing by other beasts, such as the phantom puma, may be a more likely explanation though.

Astonishingly, there is evidence that the puma has been of significance to Glasgow for some time. The Victoria infirmary opened on 14 February 1890. A long-standing mystery has been the origin of the figure carved in stone above the main entrance. It is that of a snarling puma. The puma also appears on a mosaic in the front hall and even, apparently, at one time, on badges given to nurses at graduation. There is no known origin for this strange symbol. But it is clear that for some unexplained reason the puma was, more than a century ago, recognised as having a connection to Glasgow.

It's an odd fact, but objects including animals do appear out of nowhere. This is an ancient phenomenon, but look at recent examples: in January 2007 thousands of dead birds including crows and pigeons fell out of the sky in Australia and the USA and there was no explanation for this bizarre event; in March 2007, in Edinburgh, an enormous zebra eel, usually found in the Pacific Ocean, turned up dead in a back garden following on from a report that a goldfish had suddenly dropped out of the sky during the previous month. In fact, similar events have been reported for centuries and Glasgow managed to go one better when a dead shark was found lying on a city street. How it had got there was never discovered, but it looked fresh, as if had just arrived, and was never claimed. Could there be wormholes on earth just as there are, as scientists tell us, in outer space? Wormholes connecting different parts of our world, or linking the past with the present;

gaps in the fabric of the universe through which animals enter and exit? Would this explain mysterious disappearances like those in the Bermuda Triangle? Or unsolved missing-persons cases?

It is possible to understand why the living might vanish, but why would dead bodies disappear? The 'resurrection men', active during the nineteenth century, have earned a sinister reputation. But could their motives have been of an even more bizarre nature? The idea of 'resurrection' means more than simply digging up a dead body. It suggests the intention to bring that body back to life. There's no doubt that some strange experiments were being conducted, glimpses of which have occasionally surfaced. In October 1819 the body of Matthew Clydesdale, who had been hanged for murder, was sent for dissection to Glasgow University. However, instead of cutting open the cadaver to give his medical students the opportunity to examine the interior workings of a human body, Dr James Jeffray took it upon himself, for no obvious reason, to carry out a public experiment, which he must have expected to succeed. Or why attempt it? Jeffray connected Matthew Clydesdale's body to a battery he had rigged up. He inserted air tubes connected to the battery into the subject's nostrils. The apparent reason for this was to force air into the corpse's lungs. Jeffray then activated the battery. And all hell broke loose.

Clydesdale, who had been put in a chair in a reclining position rather then lying on his back, started to move his arms and legs. His chest was heaving up and down. Witnesses related how he then opened his eyes in horror, and tried to stand up. According to one account, Jeffray, terrified by what had happened, then stabbed Clydesdale in the neck to make sure he died. Exactly what Jeffray was up to remains a mystery. Some have suggested that Clydesdale was not really dead. The execution, it is said, had been botched so he'd only been strangled then fallen unconscious. But that seems like an attempt to explain away the inexplicable. It might be asked what Jeffray had been doing to the body beforehand, and whether, instead of air, he had been pumping some other substance into Clydesdale's lungs. It's clear that Jeffray did not expect the reaction from Clydesdale that he got. But why did he kill him just as the audience were cheering his miraculous feat? When he had achieved the impossible of bringing a dead man back to life. It may be that the body had a stronger reaction than Jeffray anticipated. That he only expected the 'corpse' to start breathing, but not to react quite so forcefully. If Clydesdale started to talk what secrets might he have revealed? Following this public exhibition, Jeffray disappeared from view. But did he really stop his experiments? Information is scarce, but it would be intriguing to discover exactly what links he had to the resurrection men of the times.

In the eighteenth and nineteenth centuries a resurrection blitz hit Scottish graveyards. The notorious case of Burke and Hare has hidden a truly bizarre phenomenon. Bodies were being dug up at such a rate that guards were being employed to keep watch over the city's cemeteries. But corpses still vanished. Doubts remain that they were dug up simply for medical dissection. So many were disappearing, that could so easily be identified, that one might well ask why go to all the trouble of digging up a grave? Weren't the hospitals and poorhouses of the time full of the impoverished, family-less dead, whom no one would ever miss? Even in the twenty-first-century people disappear every day and are never heard of again. How much truer of the early nineteenth century when bureaucracy and communication were far less sophisticated?

Of course, it might be asked that if we are dealing with a phenomenon that went beyond digging up bodies for medical research, where are the grave robbers of today? Occasionally, it comes to public attention that a body has been dug up, but perhaps the answer dates from the time of the resurrection men. It was noted that graves would be opened and the bodies removed with the earth replaced so carefully that no one knew they had been taken. It was only by pure chance that the theft of a corpse was discovered. How often are graves checked up on today? No doubt resurrection men were going about their grisly business, but was that the whole story? Take a notorious case that ended up in court. Unarguably, the anatomy department at Glasgow University was using corpses for teaching and research purposes. But were these bodies those that were, surreptitiously, being dug out of the ground? A woman's corpse, that of Mrs Annette McAllister, had been removed from the Ramshorn churchyard and relatives suspected it had been taken to the university. A search of the rooms of Dr Granville Pattison in College Street revealed a number of bodies. Pattison and Andrew Russell, a lecturer in surgery at the university, were charged with 'violating' the grave of Mrs McAllister in the Ramshorn churchyard and that, in addition, they had 'her body taken to their dissecting rooms, where it was found and identified'. Both men were quickly found not guilty as it was shown that the body identified as Mrs McAllister's was not, in fact, her. She had borne children, but the corpse on which the case was built was that of a woman who had never been pregnant and might even have been a virgin. Mrs McAllister's body was never found. Pattison was not charged with any other offence so the bodies discovered in his rooms must have been legitimately received. A case that suggests bodies were being removed from graveyards for purposes other than the need of the medical profession.

Of how much use for medical purposes, in any case, was a corpse that was so old that it had been buried in the ground? By then a body had plenty of time to decompose and must have been of limited use for medical purposes. And why run the risk of getting caught having a corpse dug up when there were plenty of unidentified dead on the streets of nineteenth-century Glasgow? On the other hand, there were certain individuals who might, along with the medical profession, have an interest. One reason to dig up a dead body would be to use it for ritual purposes. The answer, in other words, could lie in magic. And black magic at that.

Dougie, a Wiccan high priest and a leading figure on the Scottish scene, on one terrifying occasion in the 1990s, found his life threatened by a gollum. A gollum is created by a black magician using either the soil from a grave or the dead body itself. The body is then 'resurrected' through a ritual and impregnated with an evil spirit, but remains under the control of the Satanist who raised it. Dougie spent the whole night crouched in a corner of his flat with the gollum standing over him. He was only saved because his sacred knife, his athame, consecrated in ritual magic, kept the gollum at bay. When the sun rose the light drove the gollum away. Like a vampire the gollum can only operate during the hours of darkness.

A gollum can be distinguished from a vampire by the fact that a vampire resembles a normal human being and can control its behaviour. A vampire needs human blood to survive whereas the gollum does not need any sustenance. The gollum is not a functioning entity in the same way as a vampire. Reports exist of people passing a graveyard and seeing a dead body come out of the ground with the appearance of a living person. This would definitely be a vampire as a gollum could not exist without the appropriate spells having been carried out.

Going by the number of reports though, vampires seem to keep a low profile, but, occasionally, alleged sightings of these entities cause a stir. In 1954 the occupants of Caledonia Road were disturbed by hundreds of children roaming a nearby cemetery, the southern necropolis. The children were searching for a vampire with iron teeth which, they claimed, had been wandering through the gravestones. It was rumoured that the vampire had killed two boys. Police called in were bombarded with descriptions from the children of what had been seen. In fact, there was no evidence that anyone, either a child or an adult, had been a victim, but there is little doubt about the strength of the rumours. And whether or not someone had, in reality, been assaulted a sighting of something weird certainly appeared to be at the bottom of it. The intruder, whoever or whatever it was, simply disappeared and, as far as is known, did not surface again. At least, not in this cemetery.

On the west side of Glasgow stands a house not haunted by a

ghost, nor plagued by any other entity, but nonetheless one that gave its occupants a very uncomfortable time. In 1997 I was called in to look over the building, situated close to the district of Loanhead which, according to the message I had received, was the source of persistent illness for the family who lived there. I had been involved, some months before, in investigating a school annexe in Ayr, which had been abandoned because of recurring ill health among staff and pupils. Officials from the education department, and health and safety, had found no explanation for the high level of sickness. However, following a dowsing survey I proposed that the problem stemmed from the confluence of ley lines. The building was alive with energy and the focus of leys on the small area occupied by the annexe had produced a huge build up of energy. There was no way to reduce the effect and the building was unusable. The only solution, I suggested, was to demolish it. A similar concentration can happen anywhere. The only surprising thing is that it doesn't occur more often. Some argue that it takes place more regularly than people recognise and that the build up of 'bad' energy around a building can explain many illnesses. So when I entered the terraced house in Loanhead I guessed that energy flow might be the issue. However, I was stunned at what I discovered. The energy level was so intense that you felt it as soon as you stepped through the door. It crackled around your skin and you could sense the disorientating affects on your mind. The whole house, a terraced building, was soaked in this adverse energy field.

Even stranger was the fact that the houses on either side were, as far as could be determined, unaffected. It was almost as if a channel of 'black' energy was coursing through this one building. The result for the occupants had been recurrent illness and sleep disturbance. Walking through the bedrooms immediately explained why. The rooms, like those on the ground floor, were throbbing with a penetrating energy that it was impossible to avoid or ignore. Tinfoil, though quite why no one seems sure, acts as a barrier to this energy so I did suggest that for sleeping purposes tinfoil placed beneath the bed might reduce the effect, though it would not be a long-term solution. Although this worked for a short time it gradually wore off and the energy levels in the bedroom became as intense as before. Other solutions tried, including an attempt to deflect the energy streams before they entered the building, also failed to reduce the 'bad' energy flow. It left many in the dowsing community mystified. One explanation was that the energy stream was too powerful because it was narrow, just as running water speeds up to create a stronger current when forced through a gorge. There had been a build up of water at the rear of the property, where there was an overflowing burn, and it was probably here that the negative energy field originated. The family eventually moved on.

Buildings often seem to have a life of their own. So what was it about the notorious 'Monkey House' near Bishopton that persuaded eccentric Glasgow entertainment magnate Albert Pickard to buy it in the 1930s but never live in it? Pickard had made a fortune from his cinema and theatre empire based in Glasgow. He had a natural interest in the bizarre and even claimed to have discovered a leprechaun in Ireland, which he displayed at one of his entertainment venues. There's no doubt that the Monkey House attracted Pickard because of its weird reputation. Its origins date back to 1901 when the millionaire stockbroker, John Holms, arranged a meeting with architect Robert Lorimer at the Glasgow International Exhibition. Holms had made a fortune from his business interests in Paisley and Glasgow and now he wanted a building people would remember him by. The result was the bizarre mansion with the name Formakin House, but known less formally as the Monkey House because of the strange-looking gargoyles – usually described as monkeys but which could just as easily be of demons – that adorn the building. However, Formakin House seemed cursed from the start. Holms bought land some miles from Glasgow and gave the estate the mysterious name 'the Field of Hares'. Hares have long been associated with witchcraft and it is claimed that part of the estate belonged at one time to two brothers who in the sixteenth century had been charged with being in league with the Devil. Locally, it was believed that the area was cursed and indeed John Holms was so battered by misfortune that, although work began on the mansion in 1911, it was never properly finished or so it was claimed. However, it did have a completed interior and, most spectacularly, a great hall. Tapestries, with mystical scenes from the time of Arthur and Merlin, were hung in the great hall, which, in addition, had three high windows and an enormous fireplace decorated with more 'monkeys' or perhaps demons and minstrels. Holms spent a fortune on the three gardens of the estate: these were the fountain, oriental and walled gardens. The gardens were joined by pathways lined with heart-shaped stones.

In 1913, Holms allegedly ran out of money and work stopped. Whether or not the mansion was 'unfinished', it lay empty, but Holms, rather strangely, lived on the estate in a cottage. So was Holms, as has been claimed, using Formakin House to carry out strange rituals? It was an era, like the present, obsessed with the power of magic and contacting the dead. Whatever the truth, its reputation as a place where strange things happened grew, especially after Holms's death in 1938, after which, it was said, his ghost haunted his beloved gardens.

Across the estate, Holms had constructed a series of buildings based on those of seventeenth-century Scotland. It seems he wanted to create a different world, one out of the past. And here another mystery arises. There has been considerable speculation over a series of stone inscriptions that can be found dotted around Formakin, which some have interpreted as a secret cipher. At the entrance to the stable yard, for example, the carved motif, '1695 DL' appears and in other places 1694 and 1698. The standard interpretation given is that the date of the building was intentionally fictitious and that 'DL' stands for 'damned lie', a joke for those in the know. Others have speculated that it is a mystic code of some kind. The numbers 1, 6 and 9, for example, can stand for the

Devil. However, 5 does not have the same significance. So is there any connection? DL could stand for the roman numerals 550, but can anything be read into that? There's little doubt that '1695 DL' and the other numbers were meant to convey something other than a date, but what it was may never be uncovered.

What Albert Pickard wanted with the building may never be known. He had no obvious link with John Holms although he did share his interest in the bizarre. It may be that he intended to use it to display some of the weirder objects he had gathered. Or he had a closer link with Holms than is known about. It is strange to buy a property with such a special character then choose not to live in it. Had Pickard bought it in good faith and then learned a secret about the place, a secret that kept him well away from the infamous Monkey House? Whatever the truth, Formakin, after lying empty for decades, was bought by property developers and converted into luxury flats. Not quite what Holms intended but at least part of his dream lived on.

A quite different fate awaited a building in the heart of the city, which was as mysterious in its way to the citizens of two hundred years ago as Formakin House is today. In Dunchattan Street, east of Glasgow cathedral, there once stood a mysterious walled building, allegedly a factory, and built in the 1770s by George Macintosh, who had arrived in the city from the Highlands. Macintosh, it was claimed, was operating a secret dyeing process and so the wall that surrounded the works and his use of Gaelic speakers was to ensure that no one could find out just what was going on inside. At the centre of the seventeen-acre plot was a mound, on which Macintosh built a big house. Understandably, rumours abounded. Just what was he and his secret coterie really engaged in? Claims of body-snatching and links to groups like the city's notorious Hellfire Club have never been substantiated. But can we truly believe that all the secrecy was simply to hide away the production of a dye? Those at the time didn't think so. We may never know the truth behind what was known as the 'secret work'. Macintosh, for unexplained reasons, suddenly abandoned the factory and, if there really were any, the secrets of life at Dunchattan Street died with him.

It was suggested that the house had been cursed and there is a long history of belief in the power of cursing, stretching back into Roman times. It may usually be associated with pagans and witches, but, in fact, the uttering of a curse was often practised by key officials of the Christian faith. In the sixteenth century, Gavin Dunbar, Bishop of Glasgow, cursed the notorious outlaws of the Scottish Borders, the thieves, sheep stealers and just plain criminals who were making life a misery for their fellow citizens. In the days before there was a police force the enforcement of justice and the ability to deal with crime was a haphazard affair. Punishment could be severe, but the chance of apprehending the guilty party was even less than it is today, so people of the time resorted to practices that might very definitely be considered on the fringe. Calling on the spirits of another world to punish Scotland's criminals was one way of tackling lawlessness. Certainly, Gavin Dunbar seems to have invoked some strange and powerful sources in putting together his curse. This was far more than a few choice insults – it was nothing less than a fifteen-hundred-word condemnation that called on supernatural forces literally to tear their bodies apart and appealed to Satan to take these lawbreakers down to hell. So powerful was the curse that its force, it is claimed, has continued down to the twenty-first century. In 2001 it was held to be responsible for the outbreak of foot-and-mouth disease in Dumfriesshire and efforts were made to have the curse lifted, four hundred years after Gavin Dunbar put it all together. Only time will tell whether the power of the Glasgow bishop's curse will finally be overturned.

Of course, if psychic forces can do harm they can also do good, as supporters of Partick Thistle FC discovered in February 1998. Thistle were having a difficult season and sat near the bottom of the league. World-renowned psychic Uri Geller offered to help manager John McVeigh and the players to improve the team's performance. Geller – who was reported to have helped several football clubs including Barcelona and some from the top division in England – invited the team to his home to benefit from his famous crystal chair. This, one would imagine, was intended to boost and cleanse each player's psychic aura, which in turn would raise confidence and improve performance on the field. It was a generous offer from Geller who, reportedly, was shocked to hear that the Firhill side could go bust if relegated. The Jags, however, turned down the great man's offer. While Geller's solution might have seemed over the top, football clubs have a history of using unorthodox measures to extend a winning streak, or to end a losing one. Several have had players hypnotised and used relaxation techniques like yoga and reiki. And England manager Glenn Hoddle famously consulted a psychic, a move that damned him in the eyes of the London media. But were Thistle right to reject Uri Geller's offer? Perhaps they should have accepted his help. At the end of the 1997/98 season Partick Thistle with thirty-six points were relegated to the second division along with Stirling Albion.

My own theory is that football success is at least partly related to the energy surrounding or crossing a football field, and this was played out against the background of Hampden Park and the national team. I offered to dowse the national stadium to determine those parts of the pitch that would boost a player's energy and those that would work against him. It has long been noted by dowsers that football grounds have often been placed, clearly without the architect being aware of it, to take account of ley lines. The focus of energy on certain parts of the playing field could, arguably, improve or worsen a player's ability in a match. How often do we hear a commentator say that more goals have been scored at one end of the park rather than the other? Is it really just coincidence? How often is it noted that a team's performance may be sparkling one week, but lethargic the next?

Fast cars and clubbing seem to go hand-in-hand. But even the city's hottest nightspot is tame compared to the activities of certain Glasgow citizens two hundred years ago. The Hellfire Club was notorious in its time, but the influence it exerted on leading figures and the extent of involvement of well-known people has still not been fully revealed. It may never be as many of its members hid their connection as details of the club's strange activities gradually spread across the land. The club was probably founded in London by Sir Francis Dashwood in the 1760s and the link between the London club and Glasgow is not clear, but in terms of activity they seemed to be on the same wavelength. Down south the Hellfire Club engaged in every kind of perverse activity including incest. Sexual orgies were held, with 'temples' set up within existing churches to carry out weird religious rites. Naked women were laid out on altars while 'priests' carried out a 'sacred' ritual. The club was fascinated with fire and may well have practised the ancient rite of fire worship. This may explain why Glasgow's Tron Kirk was set ablaze by the Hellfire Club in 1793.

Incredibly, in spite of the bizarre activities of the club it had many prominent individuals among its members. They included several well-known Scots, even the Earl of Bute, who became prime minister in the 1760s. He made the Hellfire Club founder, Francis Dashwood, his chancellor of the exchequer. Few names from the membership of the Glasgow branch have come down to us. Best known, though apparently not one of its more influential members, is Hugh Adamson. He ended up at the end of a rope in 1805, allegedly for forgery, although he had been foolish enough to return to the city after the 1793 Tron escapade. Exactly what the members of the Hellfire Club were doing in the Tron Kirk is unclear. It is likely, however, that they were carrying out one of the perverted rites that were part of the club's practice. The only indisputable fact is that the Kirk ended up being fired. This may have been an accident, but might equally have been a deliberate act. Members of the Hellfire Club had regularly burnt down buildings and had an obsession with fire. It is said that members of the club left the city after the event, though evidence for that seems slim. No attempt was made to arrest those involved who, in any case, certainly had influential contacts extending to the heart of the British establishment, including of course the prime minister and the chancellor of the exchequer. Hugh Adamson was the only person of the Glasgow Hellfire Club known to have faced a court and his fate had, on the surface, nothing to do with the events of 1793. Unless, of course, you suspect a cover up. It is possible that Adamson – who liked doing obviously outrageous things, like running through a graveyard blowing a trumpet and calling on the dead to rise – was a bit of a liability. The charge against him may have been trumped up and the rope the best way to silence this attention seeker in order to protect the powerful figures connected to him.

But did the Hellfire Club really die or did it just change shape? To take one notorious example, the Skull and Bones society has existed since 1832 and is based at Yale University in the United States. Its origins have been traced back to nineteenth-century European secret societies and strange outfits like the Hellfire Club. Skull and Bones – which has included US presidents among its members – is said to engage in bizarre rituals including fire worship and lying in a coffin in a building known as 'the Tomb'.

In fact, the worship of fire has a long history. It is not only the great destroyer, but also the conduit of change and rebirth as in the myth of the phoenix rising from the ashes. Did fire worship originate with strange phenomena seen in the sky? During May 1978 Glasgow and Clydeside were bombarded by a truly strange phenomenon. It was labelled 'lightning' because no term seemed adequate to describe the event. But for those in the thick of it, it appeared for all the world like fast-moving balls of fire shooting down from the skies. A spokesman for Glasgow Weather Centre said, 'People are convinced that they have seen fireballs, but there is little scientific information about them.' Scientists have always doubted the existence of ball lightning. Indeed in May 1978 one explanation given for the phenomenon was that it was no more than an impression left on the eye as the aftermath of a lightning bolt striking the ground. But there have been too many reported sightings of this bizarre phenomenon to dismiss it in this way.

Witnesses have reported seeing ball-shaped glowing objects, which can pass through walls, but can at the same time set objects ablaze. Even more controversial is the fact that, according to some witnesses, they are under intelligent control and move about as if searching for something. The fireballs that struck in May 1978 may have been of a different order. One that hit petrol tanks in a Blantyre garage was reported as being over six-feet wide, larger than ones usually connected to ball lightning. In Milngavie one house caught fire after a fireball struck. Fireballs and ball lightning may be separate phenomena, but, if so, where did those of 1978 come from?

And could there be a link to spontaneous human combustion (SHC), which has been a much-debated topic? The idea that a human body can suddenly burst into flames and burn like a lump of coal seems to defy the laws of nature. But it appears to happen nevertheless. There is a natural reluctance on the part of fire brigades to classify anything as not having a natural explanation, even if it cannot be identified. The accounts that I have heard over the years have been given by ex-firefighters, who have felt more able to talk. One incident took place in a tenement close to Glasgow city centre. The elderly lady was slumped in an armchair beside a single-bar electric fire. Only part of the body was burned, but almost to ashes. A blanket over her legs had been singed. The rest of the room was untouched. It didn't seem possible that such a small source of heat could have led to an intense blaze in a restricted environment. 'If we'd have said spontaneous human combustion we'd have been laughed at', I was told. The typical spontaneous-combustion incident involves a single person who, on their own, is discovered burned. In many cases there may be no report of a fire. But even where a fire is reported the limited nature of the blaze raises questions over why the person within a room suffered so badly. In Glasgow, fires occurring leaving a lone victim dead, but the cause of the fire 'unknown', are a regular event.

Some people who have survived SHC describe a blue flame appearing on an arm or a leg, which then spreads rapidly across the body. And it doesn't necessarily happen in the home. Incidents have been reported in schools and even out in the open. So does it come from inside us or from the heavens like a bizarre bolt of mini-lightning?

For some years I was in touch with an individual who claimed that he could predict these events. They were, in his view, related to 'earth energy forces' and other factors, including the movement of the planets. This was a 'scientific' attempt to explain strange and random events. But psychics can do the same thing simply by the power of the mind. And there appears to be a bit of psychic ability in all of us. A young man at Glasgow University, Thomas Walters, had a dream in which he learnt that his aunt had passed over. Soon after, news arrived that his aunt had died on the day he had had the dream; this was an unusual, but by no means unique, paranormal experience. But these incidents can be even more complicated. A Glasgow businessman had a dream in which he saw the corpse of a friend lying in a coffin. The name of his friend was carved on the side with the date of his death. Later he learnt that his friend had died and when the businessman attended the funeral the date on the coffin was the same as the one he had seen in his dream. To dream of the death of a friend or relative may not necessarily be unusual, but when that dream gives or coincides with an exact date then it is harder to explain away.

Other incidents appear even more complex, including one I was told about in the 1980s by Andy Busby of Cambuslang. It was bizarre yet compelling, so much so that I later wrote about it for the magazine, *Phenomenal News*. In 1956 Mr Busby, then aged forty, was in the habit of taking a regular after-dinner stroll along the banks of the Clyde. He often passed a spot where families gathered and young children would paddle in the water. One summer evening, as Andy passed by, he caught sight of a youngster walking further and further out till the water was above his waist and the current started to grow in strength, buffeting him from side to side. The lad, who looked about six years old, turned, stared directly at Andy, then suddenly disappeared from view. Andy reacted immediately, shouting for help and running towards the water. He ploughed into the river struggling towards the spot where he'd last seen the lad. But there was no sign of him. By now people had come running over and were asking what had happened. They were startled when Andy explained what he'd seen. No one else had witnessed the incident or even the boy who, Andy told them, had been wearing a distinctive red top and carrying a white ball. Other children, who'd been paddling at the time, swore that the boy had never been there. Andy staggered home soaking wet, wondering if his mind was playing tricks. He felt embarrassed about the whole thing and had some explaining to do to his wife.

But he couldn't get the image of the drowning boy out of his head. The incident kept coming back to him as a recurring dream. For several weeks Andy avoided his usual walk, but something was pulling him back. So one evening he decided to retrace his footsteps. As he came to the spot by the river it was as if his 'dream' was being replayed. It looked exactly like the wee lad Andy had seen in his vision those weeks before, standing at the same spot in the water, wearing the same red top and holding a white ball. But this time the boy dropped the ball and as it sped away the lad made to go after it. Despite his earlier experience Andy reacted immediately. Something in his head told him that this was for real. He ran towards the river shouting to the boy to come back to the bank. The boy seemed startled, even scared, but walked away from the deeper water towards Andy and back onto dry land. Andy was aware that a small crowd had gathered wondering what was going on. 'There's a dangerous current there,' Andy explained, 'someone could easily be swept away.' He wasn't sure if the bystanders were convinced, but he wasn't bothered. All he knew was that his disturbing 'vision' hadn't come to pass and the boy had been saved. That was all he cared about. Some years later Andy was recounting the tale to a friend he hadn't met for a while, who told him that a childhood friend of his mother's had drowned near that spot, an event that must have occurred in the early years of the twentieth century. Had Andy somehow tuned in to an incident from the past? A tragic event that had somehow been imprinted onto the physical surroundings? Or could it be linked to another strange story connected to the Clyde? The water kelpie, that strange half-horse, half-human creature, that is said to emerge from rivers and lochs to drag the unsuspecting down isn't confined to the Highlands. A similar creature was said to haunt the Clyde, but unlike its Highlands counterpart was more of a water spirit and would warn people of potential danger on the river. Could it have been the spirit of this water sprite that alerted Andy?

Sometimes incidents are so odd that they defy categorisation. Are we dealing with a ghost? A poltergeist? A doppelganger? Or a vision into another dimension or reality? Take the unsolved murder case, perpetrated on Glasgow Green, which was brought to public attention by Scotland's first paranormal investigator, Catherine Crowe, in her book *The Night Side of Nature*, published in 1848. There is no doubt that it clearly illustrates the links between the supernatural and our daily lives. It is an event that has never been satisfactorily explained and one the authorities tried to hush up. The names of those involved are uncertain, but the main participants have come down to us simply as John and Annie.

In the 1780s John was an assistant to a well-known surgeon of the time. His girlfriend Annie was a servant. One day Annie did not appear at work and just disappeared. This was not seen as suspicious. The couple were not married and it was believed that, a sign of the times, she had fallen pregnant and had run away to have the baby.

In the late eighteenth century Glasgow Green was, like today, a popular place to meet at weekends, but, at the time when these events occurred, there was still pressure to attend church on a Sunday.

Church representatives would look out for their members and take a note of those who were sunning themselves rather than sitting in a church pew. It was at Glasgow Green that these men came across John the surgeon's assistant, whose girlfriend Annie had disappeared. The churchmen tackled John for an explanation as to why, as a church member, he was not at Sunday service. Instead of replying John pointed in the direction of the river and said, 'look in the water'. He then got up, walked to a stile and, crossing it, took the path towards Rutherglen Road along the river bank.

When the churchmen went to the river they discovered the body of a woman floating in the water. They pulled the body out and with help from others carried it into the town. Here they received a further shock. As they passed their church the congregation was coming out and among the crowd was the same man, John, they had been talking to a little while before. The very one they had confronted on the Green. When police examined the woman's body it was identified as Annie, the missing servant girl. The murder weapon, a medical knife, was found embedded in her clothes. Her boyfriend, John, was the obvious suspect having been seen on the Glasgow Green and having directed the church people to the spot where her body was found. However, there was a problem with this 'obvious' explanation. At the time the churchmen claimed to have met him, there were dozens of other witnesses who swore that John had been occupying his usual seat in church. Clearly, he couldn't be in two places at once. So had they encountered a ghost on the Green? If so, whose ghost? And was this ghost trying to implicate the 'real' John in a murder? And if so why? Maybe there are spirits in other dimensions who try to make sure that good triumphs over evil. But, if that's true, in this case they failed because no one was ever charged with Annie's murder.

Near-death experiences support the view that there are 'other worlds' beyond our own. Retired civil servant Robert Wilson told me:

I was walking along a Glasgow street when I felt this searing pain in my chest. I can remember a crowd of faces around me and the ambulance siren; then everything seemed to go dark. Then I seemed to be floating above the pavement looking down on myself and the people standing beside me. A misty tunnel opened in front of me and I seemed to be sucked into it. At the end of the tunnel was a very bright light. There was a person standing in the light. I don't think I recognised him, but clearly remember seeing him. Then there was a voice in my head that seemed to say 'go back' or 'you're going back'. The next thing I woke up in the ambulance as we got to the hospital.

Having investigated psychic phenomena for over thirty years I can candidly state there is an endless production line of unrelated, odd events. It's no surprise some are convinced that we live in a Joker's Universe, where nothing is what it seems and in which a 'puppet master' likes to play senseless tricks on us all. Some incidents are so strange that there can be no other explanation. In 1992 Jenny Hill had her car stolen from a Glasgow street and reported the theft to the police. The following day two plain-clothes individuals turned up at her work and asked to speak to her. They were shown to her office. She noticed that they were carrying a black plastic bag and she wondered what the visitors wanted. She was surprised to learn that the two, a man and a woman, were from Strathclyde Police. They told Jenny that they knew about the theft of her car and claimed they had found it. The police explained that the plastic bag they had with them contained items from the vehicle and, without asking for permission, emptied the contents onto the floor. Jenny was dumbfounded by this, and by what came tumbling out of the bag. She said, 'It was just rubbish. It had nothing to do with my car whatsoever. I couldn't understand what was happening. I asked them to clear up the mess and leave.' They went, but after they had gone Jenny became more and more puzzled. What on earth had been going on? She decided to ring the police. They were equally surprised. They knew nothing of the individuals and could not understand what they had been up to. Jenny's car hadn't even been found. So who on earth were these individuals claiming to be from the police? And how did they know about Jenny's stolen car? Was it some weird prank being played by entities from another dimension? It's an incident so strange that it defies logic. Unsettling too, but not as frightening as the event experienced by David Thom.

In January 1983 David Thom, who was then sixty-four, was returning from the city centre to his home on the outskirts of Glasgow, driving along Dumbarton Road. A former business colleague had been spending the evening at David's home and afterwards David had taken him back to the city-centre hotel where his friend had been speaking at a training conference. It was a typical midweek night so there wasn't much traffic, especially as it was now approaching midnight. But even so, as he passed through the city suburbs, David was surprised to find that he had the road to himself. It was at a spot shortly after he had passed Kilbowie – David was never sure exactly where – that he noticed the figure on a straight stretch of road. Astonishingly, the figure was hovering a few feet above the kerb, without any visible means of support. At first David thought his eyes were deceiving him, but as he drew nearer it was clear that they weren't. The figure appeared to be glowing. David later explained:

I thought it must be a trick of the light, but as I drew parallel with the figure I couldn't have any more doubt. He or 'it' was glowing like a luminous ball. I was mesmerised and looked directly at it. It looked straight into my face. I should say that the whole figure looked human and so did the face, but sort of animal like. The worst thing was that he looked at me with sheer hatred, that's the only way I can describe it. My head started to swim, but I managed to keep my foot on the accelerator and drove past. When I looked in the mirror it was running after me and spark-like things seemed to be spraying from it in all directions. It was moving at an incredible speed and I was panicking at the thought that it might catch up with me. I've never felt so scared in all my life. After what seemed like an age, but was probably only a few seconds, a car came along on the other side of the road and when I looked in the mirror again the figure had gone. It was a few days before I drove that way at night again trying to see whether it had been a trick of the light which had set off something in my imagination? Or had I been half dozing in the car and experienced some kind of waking dream? I haven't heard of anything like it on the road before or since. If it hadn't happened to me I don't think I would have believed it.

David's experience begs the question. Just exactly what kind of world are we living in? Does Glasgow lie on the edge of some weird 'other dimension' where anything is possible? Or are these isolated incidents designed to baffle us and which, quite simply, will never be satisfactorily explained? An inevitable by-product of living in Scotland's most mysterious city.

# 6

# Witchcraft and Satanism

I spoke to a Glasgow man who called himself Astaroth several times in the course of research for my 'X-Files' column in the *Evening Times*. In psychic lore Astaroth is an evil spirit who takes his orders from Satan. But I wasn't contacting a spirit from another world. This was very much a human being, but one who didn't want his name broadcast so asked to be called after one of the occult's best-known demons. It was the pseudonym he used in the circles he moved in, though he denied that his adopted name had any sinister implications. Several years on and I'm still not sure whether Astaroth told a convincing story, but it was certainly an intriguing one. He claimed that he was from a long line of Glasgow witches stretching back hundreds of years. He told me in confidence that his ancestors had been executed during the great witch trials of the past. But witchcraft, he said, had never died out and there were still covens active within the city. In fact, they were flourishing. They held ceremonies outdoors. But you would be unlikely to stumble across them because they were held at the dead of night in secret spots. Sometimes these were in areas sacred to witches, locations in which the special power necessary to perform magic rites could be generated, but as often at a spot where no one else would consider walking late at night. Astaroth hinted there was a network of individuals in Glasgow involved in witchcraft, but never offered firm proof. I questioned him about lurid tales of babies being sacrificed and young virgins used as human altars in weird sexual rites. Stories splashed across the front pages of the press at this time. He denied it as far as white witches were concerned, but did agree that those using black magic and on the extreme fringe of the occult could be less scrupulous. Wild tales, he admitted, circulated, but it was difficult to separate fact from fiction. I came to no conclusion about Astaroth, but part of his story certainly rang true. It is undeniable that Glasgow has a long history as a centre of the occult and recently has been awash with strange events that could be linked to witchcraft.

Horses slashed as part of a bizarre ritual. Sightings of men and women dancing naked on a hillside, performing weird ceremonies and carving pentagrams in the grass. Skulls and other strange objects left in a graveyard. Could this mean that there are witches active in Glasgow today? And could there be a secret society of witches whose roots stretch back hundreds of years into a pagan past? An occult underground that has succeeded in keeping its activities hidden from public gaze? At the height of the witchcraft craze, when men and women of all ages were being burnt alive, that would not have been a hard question to answer. Witches were people who had sold their soul to the Devil and in return were given supernatural powers, which they would use against their neighbours. Men and women were struck down by sudden illness. Babies died at birth. Crops and cattle were destroyed. Anyone rich or poor was at risk from a servant of the Devil. In a series of witch-craft panics that spread across Scotland at intervals during the seventeenth century two landmark cases stand out. Both test to the limit the sceptics' view that belief in the reality of Satan is little more than a delusion. Bizarre incidents occurred in front of many witnesses, and individuals involved in satanic activities confessed, without any pressure, to forging a pact with the Devil. So are we too ready to deny the existence of Satan and witchcraft? Too willing to ignore the evidence that the Devil and his followers are still active, operating unnoticed within the precincts of the city?

The first case reverberated across Scotland and involved a well-known figure from Glasgow, who moved in the country's best social circles. It struck fear into the hearts of many ordinary Scots that so prominent a person as Sir George Maxwell – whose ancestors had been major landowners for centuries, and regarded themselves as the equal of any king of Scotland – could be the victim of a Satanic plot. But the evidence seemed to speak for itself. On 14 October 1676, Maxwell, who owned Pollok estate, where Pollok Hall now stands, set out for a business meeting in Glasgow city centre. Soon after he arrived he was struck down by a sudden illness. Sweat poured from him and he complained of racking chest pains. He was carried back to Pollok Hall, but appeared to have lost all energy. He told doctors that he felt as if he was being repeatedly stabbed by a dagger down his left side.

But this mystery illness soon turned into something more sinister. Teenager Janet Douglas had arrived in the city from the Highlands in 1676 giving demonstrations of her psychic ability. She told a goldsmith that his business was being ruined because some evil-minded person had secreted a clay statue in his shop. The shopkeeper's name had been carved on the image, cursed and left there in a deliberate attempt to drive trade away by magic. When the man went to his shop he found the clay model there, just as Janet had predicted. Janet's reputation was assured from that moment on.

She became friendly with Anne and Marie Maxwell, Sir George Maxwell's daughters, and became a regular visitor to their home. Learning of Sir George's unexplained illness Janet Douglas claimed that Janet Mathie, a local widow, was attempting to murder Maxwell by witchcraft. In a vision she had seen Mathie make a wax figure and then stick pins into it, at the same time chanting a witch's spell to activate the magic. Laurence Pollok and Andrew Martin, who worked for Maxwell, followed her to the Mathie house. Inside Janet Douglas went to the fireplace and pulled out a wax figure from behind the grate. A pin had been pushed into both sides. Andrew Martin showed the find to John Maxwell, Sir George's son, who had Janet Mathie imprisoned in the local gaol.

John Maxwell believed that the Mathie family had good reason for enlisting the forces of the occult in an attack on his father. Sir George had threatened to arrest Hugh, Janet Mathie's son, who had been stealing from him. He had made the threat on the same day,

14 October, that he fell ill. It was suspected that Janet was using witchcraft against Maxwell as revenge. She had a longstanding reputation for being involved with the 'Black Arts'.

Janet Mathie protested that Janet Douglas had planted the evidence and made up the witchcraft story. But was that true? Some believed her, but to others it was a case of 'she would say that wouldn't she'. Meanwhile, Janet Mathie was stripped and every part of her naked body was thoroughly searched for a blemish or reddened area of the skin. They were looking for the 'Devil's Mark', put there by Satan to seal the pact with his servants, like cattle branded on the farm. It was well known that the Devil liked to put the mark where it was not obviously seen, especially around the vagina, so that those looking for it had to make a special search around the sexual organs. The blushes of the accused were not spared as the gaolers went about their business.

In spite of hours of interrogation Mathie held to her story and continued to deny ever having been a witch. Unfortunately for her, however, George Maxwell had been feeling better since the discovery of the wax figure. So she was left in gaol where, it was believed, she would eventually break down and confess.

Soon after the new year of 1677 Maxwell took a turn for the worse. Janet Douglas explained that Janet's son, John Mathie, had made a wax figure of Sir George and hidden it beneath his bed. While Janet waited outside, Maxwell's servants searched the cottage. Under the straw mattress they found a clay figure shaped like a man, with three pins pressed into it.

Mathie claimed that he had never set eyes on the clay figure before. But, despite protesting his innocence, he was arrested with his fourteen-year-old sister, Annabel, and charged with witchcraft. Annabel admitted her involvement. She claimed that Satan himself had gathered a group of followers including her brother John, and local women Bessie Weir, Margery Craig and Margaret Jackson. They had met at her mother's house in early January 1677, where they had made the model of George Maxwell.

John was now searched and marks were found on his body which, it was believed, could only have been put there by the Devil. News then arrived that Maxwell had made an astonishing recovery. Was this simply coincidence? Or a case of coincidence too far? John Mathie crumbled and admitted that he had made a pact with Satan and moulded the wax figure of Sir George.

There were those who agreed with Janet Mathie that Janet Douglas had planted the wax models. It was certainly possible. But Janet made a fresh accusation. She claimed that in a vision she had seen Janet Mathie make another wax figure and hide it beneath the bed in her cell. A search of the cell on 17 January confirmed what the Douglas girl had said. The model was found where she had predicted it would be. So did Janet have an accomplice or were her visions truly supernatural? And were there really witches?

The trial of the accused opened on 27 January 1677. It was revealed that the coven involved in attacking Maxwell had been set up forty years earlier when Margaret Jackson, now in her eighties, encountered the Devil while walking in Eastwood. She couldn't remember exactly what he'd said, she explained, but by the end of their conversation she had renounced Christianity and agreed to become his servant. Some time later Bessie Weir and Janet Mathie joined the coven. Annabel Mathie added that when Satan visited their cottage he came, 'in the shape of a black man . . . his apparel was black . . . his feet were cloven . . . and he had hoggers on his legs'. Annabel agreed to become his servant only after Bessie and her mother persuaded her to do so. She then performed the rite of submission, putting one hand on the crown of her head and the other to the sole of her foot, giving all in between to the strange entity. The Devil then took Annabel to the bed where they had sex together. She described the sensation as piercing cold inside her.

The plot to kill Maxwell was hatched soon after one evening in October at Janet Mathie's. They made a wax figure, put it on a spit over a fire and turned it, chanting all the time 'George Maxwell, George Maxwell'. Then just as the flames started to melt the image,

Sir George, who was in the city centre, experienced the first agonising pains in his chest.

John Mathie told the court that Bessie Weir was Satan's most trusted adviser. She turned up at John's door in January 1677 and reported that the 'Master' had ordered the remaining witches to meet at Janet's house, where a fresh wax model was made of Sir George. This was the figure found in John's bed following Janet Douglas's vision. John admitted his motive was revenge, which the Devil had promised him if he joined the coven. Revenge had also turned Bessie Weir against Maxwell, as he had refused to employ her husband during harvest time.

While Margaret Jackson, John and Annabel Mathie readily admitted their guilt, the other accused – Bessie Weir, Janet Mathie and Margery Craig – protested their innocence. But only Annabel Mathie escaped the death penalty. The rest were sentenced to be burned at the stake.

Janet Douglas meanwhile was making fresh accusations. She claimed that she had discovered more members of the coven, and had seen them present at 'sabbats', general gatherings of Satan's followers where obscene rites were carried out. She named several prominent local women. But they had considerably more clout than Janet Mathie and no action was taken against them. Was Janet Douglas speaking the truth though? Was there a coven of witches that included prominent people? Why would Janet take the risk of implicating them if she didn't believe in her visions? Had down-and-out figures like Bessie Weir been sacrificed to cover up the activities of others? The Maxwell family dropped Janet Douglas like a hot potato. But she remained a popular figure with the public, who believed in her power of 'second sight'.

In spite of the fact that it had been her 'visions' that had sent several women to their death as witches, Janet ended up in an Edinburgh gaol well away from events in Glasgow. The explanation was that her claimed supernatural powers and accusation of witch-craft were likely to excite the mob. Others had a more sinister explanation. She was locked up to shut her up. To keep the real witches safe.

One of those who came to interview her was the well-known Glasgow scholar, George Hickes. He described his meeting in letters to the great English diarist, Samuel Pepys. Janet was by this time behaving like a twenty-first-century celebrity, granting interviews only to a favoured few. Hickes gained a favourable impression of her and wrote that she had a 'bold, undaunted spirit'. She refused, however, to talk about her background and all that could be learned was that she came originally from the Scottish Highlands, or so she claimed, where she had first earned a reputation for 'second sight'. Hickes, no fool, was so taken by her that he told Pepys, 'People were divided in their opinion. Some believed her to be simply an impostor, but others, I myself being one, thought that she really was what she claimed to be. I came to that view from facts which even the most sceptical could hardly deny.' These 'facts' were visions experienced by Janet of Hickes's own life, and which he confirmed were largely accurate.

In spite of his faith in Janet's supernatural abilities Hickes did doubt her claims about her Highland origins as she spoke English so well. He told her of his suspicions, but Janet ignored him. Hickes believed that Janet was the illegitimate daughter of a person of 'honour and quality', a view reinforced after she was unexpectedly set free. Hickes believed that secret supporters at a high level were helping her. Janet vanished shortly after. It was suggested that she had been transported to Jamaica or North America, though to some that was just a cover story and her secret supporters had whisked her away to a hiding place. Whatever the truth, she was never seen again.

The Maxwell case is certainly puzzling. It encapsulates the whole mystery of witchcraft. Individuals admitted to being witches. They described in detail their meetings with the weird stranger, the Devil. And these confessions were made voluntarily without any physical torture. Several of those arrested protested their innocence to the end and more than likely were not involved. But others, at the very least, appear to have taken part in strange activities. Janet Douglas was right. Wax images were being made in order to harm people by magic. There is evidence for this practice from across the globe, from ancient times to the present. In the 1320s people were put on trial for using witchcraft against Edward II of England by pushing pins into wax models. But in a sense this was witchcraft at second hand. What of those events when the Devil and his demons launched a full-scale personal assault?

In September 1696 Glasgow doctor Matthew Brisbane and Henry Marshall, a chemist, were faced with a puzzling case. The eleven-year-old girl in Brisbane's surgery was displaying the strangest symptoms. She was contorted as if an invisible force had twisted her head and body into bizarre positions. Her name was Christine Shaw and she was the daughter of John Shaw, the laird of Bargarran. Shaw was a man of some local standing and completely baffled by the events that had brought Christine into Brisbane's care. Brisbane would have been astonished to learn this was to turn into one of Scotland's bloodiest witchcraft cases.

Christine had been suffering for several weeks from strange fits following an argument with Katherine Campbell, a family servant. On Monday, 17 August 1696 Christine caught Katherine about to steal a cup of milk and threatened to tell her mother of the incident. Katherine had retorted, 'The Devil drag your soul through hell.' But the incident had ended there. A few days later an old woman, Agnes Naismith, who had a reputation for threatening people and making them ill as a result, wandered into the courtyard of the Bargarran house where Christine was sitting with her newly born sister. Agnes started to chat to Christine, inquiring about the baby, but though Christine let her irritation show with Agnes's questions little else passed between them and Agnes eventually drifted off. From these unconnected and seemingly minor incidents several people were eventually to lose their lives.

The day after her chat with Agnes, Christine Shaw suddenly

floated off her bed and literally flew across the room to crash against the closed door. She complained of violent stabbing pains but would then lie stiff like a corpse for hours. Next, her body bent into the strangest positions. One day Christine started rolling about her bed apparently fighting an invisible attacker. She claimed that the spectres of Katherine Campbell and Agnes Naismith were in the room trying to kill her. John Shaw was both mystified and alarmed. Could his daughter be suffering from a bizarre illness? He decided to get medical advice and Christine was sent to Dr Brisbane in Glasgow. It seemed to do the trick. Her strange behaviour stopped and after several days, seemingly 'cured', she was sent home.

But she had hardly crossed the threshold when the weird fits returned. Matters reached the level of the bizarre when Christine began coughing up strange objects. Large quantities of knotted hair in a variety of colours came out of her mouth.

Her parents took her back to Dr Brisbane on 17 November 1696. What Brisbane saw defies natural explanation. Out of Christine's mouth came bones, pins and a variety of objects. When Archibald Bannatyne, an associate of Brisbane, tried to pull out the leg bone of a duck that had caught in Christine's mouth as she was coughing it up he felt a force pulling it back down her throat, as if something inside Christine was holding on to it.

In the days that followed she brought up candles, egg shells and, strangest of all, dung mixed with straw. Christine found the taste unbearable. Cinders, the size of chestnuts, shot from her mouth and landed with a distinct hiss on the floor. Brisbane found the lumps so hot that he could hardly hold them. Far hotter, he testified, than could be made by the human body alone. In between the coughing fits Christine seemed perfectly healthy. The events were witnessed by people from across Glasgow, who came to the surgery to view the bizarre spectacle. Her invisible attackers, meanwhile, returned. Christine appeared to be involved in a war of words with the 'spirit' of Katherine Campbell, whom she tried to persuade to abandon her pact with the Devil.

Was it being away from home in the company of Brisbane and Marshall that calmed young Christine down? On 8 December she returned to her parents and for several days it was all quiet. But then it started all over again. She had visions of the Devil, who threatened to eat her.

It had no doubt occurred to some that these incidents might simply be in Christine's mind. But on 17 December an event took place that suggested some genuinely odd incidents were happening. Christine had claimed that several people, visible only to her, were standing at her bed and shouted that she had hold of an attacker's sleeve. A cry was followed by the sound of tearing cloth. When Christine opened her hand there were shreds of a red material on her palm. A search of the room, then the whole house, revealed nothing to match. It was as a result of this incident that John Shaw, Christine's father, started to believe that his daughter might indeed be under psychic attack from a coven of witches.

Meanwhile, the strange incidents continued. Visiting church Christine accidentally dropped a glove which, in full view of the congregation, shot back into her hand, in defiance of the laws of nature. Christine again levitated out of her bed. Her brothers and sisters were walking back from the basement when they came across Christine floating down the stairs towards them, a space clearly visible between her feet and the ground. They grabbed hold of her nightdress, but she was moving with such force that it was ripped from their hands. Alexander King, the minister at Bonhill church, hearing screams, rushed to help. Holding her tightly he pulled her down all the while fighting, as he later described, an invisible entity that seemed determined to force her into the basement.

Throughout January Christine continued to spew up a variety of objects and complained of the many cats and birds lying on the bed sheets which made it hard for her to breathe. Pure fantasy? When her mother lifted the girl from her bed she glimpsed a bundle, about the size of a cat, moving beneath the blankets. But when she whipped off the cover there was nothing there.

In February twelve people were arrested on suspicion of witch-craft. A testimony to the fears that had been generated by Christine's bizarre experiences. Most, but not all, had been seen by Christine in her visions. Others had already earned notoriety as suspected followers of the Devil. Several members of one family were included in the roundup: John Anderson, his daughter Elizabeth, along with her grandmother Jean Fulton. Jean had a reputation as a witch, and her 'magic' was believed to have killed several people. Also imprisoned were Margaret Lang, her daughter Martha Semple aged eighteen, and Katherine Campbell, the Shaw family's own maidservant. Events now gathered pace. Katherine Campbell and James Lindsay were brought to the Bargarran house. No sooner did each, as instructed, touch Christine when she threw a severe fit. Clearly amazed, Katherine cried out, 'The Lord God of heaven bless thee and save thee body and soul.'

Everyone now came under suspicion. Thomas Lindsay, about Christine's age, was imprisoned on 6 February after claiming to be the son of the Devil, with the power to turn into a bird whenever he pleased. He confessed to forging a pact with Satan, who had burnt a mark on his body in confirmation of their deal. With his brother James he had attended several witch meetings presided over by Satan, in person. James, it turned out, was the 'squint-eyed elf' Christine had seen during one of her visions. He was discovered in the Glasgow tolbooth where he had been imprisoned as a vagabond. When questioned, James readily admitted that he was a witch.

He confessed that he'd first met the Devil at the house of Jean Fulton, his grandmother, where he appeared as an ordinary, but serious-looking gentleman. Jean introduced him to Satan who asked him if he would agree to serve him. 'Yes, I'll do it', replied James without hesitating and from then on he frequently attended secret meetings of the coven, each time with the Devil presiding. The sharp pains Christine experienced were due, he explained, to a magic needle in his possession, which he simply pressed against his body to produce the agony experienced by Christine in exactly the same spot.

On 8 February, Elizabeth Anderson was interrogated. Her statements corroborated the accusations of Christine Shaw. Around the middle of January, Elizabeth reported, her father took her at noon to the Bargarran courtyard where they met with 'a black man who had a bonnet on his head and a band about his neck'. Agnes Naismith then arrived and explained that the stranger was the Devil, her Master. Others present, according to Elizabeth, were the Lindsay brothers and Margaret Fulton. The five witches then discussed the best way to kill Christine, eventually agreeing to carry out their plan 'by the stopping of her breath'. A dance of celebration then followed in John Shaw's orchard, at which they toasted the success of their plan. The gathering dispersed, but not before Elizabeth's father warned her not to mention the events.

Elizabeth described her involvement in a horrific orgy of evil that included the murder of several new-born babies, visits to her grandmother's house by the Devil and plots to kill two church ministers including Alexander King of Bonhill. She said that at the meeting in Bargarran's orchard the Devil fed them on liver torn from an unbaptised child to ensure that they would never confess. Elizabeth, however, avoided eating hers so the spell could not take effect and she could now confess quite freely.

These confessions did not immediately stop the attacks on Christine. In fact, in the short run, they seemed to intensify and she experienced more visions, which reached a climax on 23 March when the Devil appeared to her. She described him as no different from an ordinary man, but with hairy hands and a face covered in thick bristles. For an hour they argued while her parents looked on, confused as ever by the tirade directed by their daughter at a bare wall. And when Christine abruptly stopped talking there was no sign that events had run their course. But, in fact, the attack on Christine by the forces of the occult had come to an end.

She recovered quickly, but the events she had sparked into action were less easy to stop. Intense efforts were made to persuade those who denied being witches to admit their guilt. Prickers, hired to test the accused, located the insensitive areas called the Devil's mark, on all members of the coven except Margaret Fulton. A witness described the scene:

> A needle of three inches length was put in without their feeling any sensation nor would any blood come from these places and although many, especially doctors, ridiculed these stories yet after we called Dr Brisbane and Dr Baird and let them see a needle of great length put into the top of one of the vertebrae of the back and one into Margaret Lang, a handbreadth beneath her ribs in the region of the lower belly, they both thought it astonishing, being in a place where in another woman the needle could not but pierce the guts.

But there was much sympathy for Margaret's daughter, Martha Semple, even though the lass was a suspected witch. The eighteen-year-old was first searched for the mark and when nothing could be found was taken to a private room where she suffered the indignity of being stripped naked. Then while justices, lawyers and ministers looked on the pricker probed her genitals for the sign that would confirm her witchcraft. 'She was the only person amongst them all that ever I saw weep', records a witness.

The trial began on 2 May, but the chances of acquittal were hardly raised by the mysterious death of one of the accused, who was being held in solitary confinement. He was discovered one evening, crouched in a chair with a cord pulled tightly round his neck. It was rumoured that the Devil had killed him before he talked too freely. What is puzzling is that the name of the man who died was never revealed. It is said that it could have been an individual of standing. A person those in authority suspected of being a ringleader, but had no wish to see put on trial, and so was silenced by them.

The fifteen jurors took seven hours to reach their decision.

Margaret Lang, her daughter Martha Semple, eighteen-year-old Katherine Campbell, the elderly Agnes Naismith and fourteen-year-old James Lindsay were sentenced to death. The sentence was carried out on 10 June 1698: the convicted witches were hung then their bodies were burnt.

Christine Shaw lived on to marry, but never, as far as is known discussed these bizarre events. There were rumours that she had put it all into a diary, which was hidden in a 'secret place'. If that is true it has never been discovered. Whether it lies under some floorboards in a long-forgotten building waiting to be found only time will tell. One of the odd aspects of this case is that the Shaw family were no strangers to 'unexplained' events. Thirty years earlier John Shaw's father had gone missing in circumstances never satis-factorily resolved. It was believed that he had drowned crossing a river and his body washed away. It had seemed just a tragic accident, until the body was discovered months later. It had been terribly, though precisely, mutilated. The genitals and right hand had been carefully sliced off. A strange ritual? Witchcraft was certainly suspected. Equally puzzling was the fact that his appearance was not that of a decaying corpse, but of someone who had only recently died. Furthermore, his clothes had been carefully folded and looked as if they had been put there only a short time before. He certainly hadn't drowned as had previously been suspected. Papers found in his pockets were dry and had, quite obviously, not been soaked in water. Nor had his hat. When his leg was pulled from his boot blood oozed from a cut in his heel, as if it had been made quite recently. So where had he been and what had happened during the time that had passed since his disappearance? No one ever got to the bottom of it. It remains an unsolved mystery. There might, of course, be no connection with the events surrounding Christine Shaw. But it is a reasonable guess that there was more going on beneath the surface than anyone was prepared to admit.

Despite the apparent deep-rooted belief in the existence of witches, witchcraft trials ceased within thirty years of the Christine

Shaw case. The mass of the people might have been convinced of the power of evil, and in the ability of certain people to use that to harm their neighbours, but the educated had come to regard it as sheer superstition, or so it was claimed. The witch, to all intents and purposes, ceased to exist and Glasgow, supposedly, was free of witchcraft. At least till the twentieth century dawned. By the 1950s witchcraft had re-emerged. By a strange irony it was the educated who were in the forefront of 'Wicca', as it was now called. To twenty-first-century witches Wicca is a pagan religion, which, its followers claim, has nothing to do with the Devil. Wiccans reject the notion that witches in previous centuries were involved in a satanic pact. They were, they argue, followers of an ancient tradition. One that celebrated the pagan gods of the distant past.

So did 'witchcraft' exist as an underground religion run by members of the upper classes? Some argue that the 'devil' who visited Bessie Weir and others was a man; the local 'priest' dressed in animal skins. The 'black man' – meaning one who wears dark clothes – who egged them on to acts of magic. And these 'priests' of the occult came, allegedly, from the best social circles. So when the heat was on, rank-and-file members were sacrificed in witch trials while their educated leaders escaped. In a further twist to this conspiracy theory it is claimed that to protect those in the upper reaches of society, the Scottish government abandoned witch trials and discredited the whole witch belief. Meanwhile, in secret, the covens, protected from the public eye, continued to flourish.

Today's Wiccans, however, seem on the face of it a far cry from the feared evildoers of the past. In the early 1990s a young woman calling herself the High Priestess of Glasgow's Pagans was reported as saying that: 'Paganism is a nature-based religion. If you've always felt an affinity with nature, and kinship with animals, you could class yourself as a pagan. It's basically about being a good person and remembering whatever you give out comes back to you three-fold.' Understandably, in the light of this bland, catch-all approach, it was also reported that 'there's nothing that annoys Wiccans more than being linked to the traditional image of evil cauldron stirrers and Satanists'.

But is this the whole picture? Wiccans, Satanists and black magicians may see themselves on separate paths to enlightenment, but that there is an overlap between those involved cannot be denied. Small though their numbers may be a number of incidents suggest that there is something strange taking place on the fringes of Glasgow society.

It may come as no surprise to learn that by the 1990s Glasgow had been branded the 'satanic city'. According to a report in the *Glaswegian* of 14 April 1990, a Christian counselling group claimed that there was evidence of 'very large satanic groups in Glasgow', which were 'very sophisticated and have a recruitment campaign that can only be described as sinister'. There had been, they claimed, eight victims of occult and ritual abuse within the previous two-year period.

In Govan a church minister also claimed at the same time that he had helped people who had been victims of ritual abuse. He told of a woman, aged thirty, who had been 'badly abused as a member of an occultist group'. By the time she left the cult her mind had been broken. In fact, she had become a physical wreck 'through her experience of witchcraft'. He also cited another incident in which a woman was encouraged by friends to attend coffee mornings and it was through these meetings that she was gradually introduced to occult practices. It suggested that an underground network existed that was secretly recruiting unsuspecting individuals to the 'craft'.

These warnings were delivered before the notorious events in Orkney in February 1991 when several adults, including a Church of Scotland minister, were accused of being involved in a satanic ring that practised ritual abuse. The arrest of those involved exploded across the media. It revealed an increasing concern about the alleged growth of Satanist activity. As Scotland's metropolis Glasgow seemed a likely place for Satanists to be carrying out their activities. It has a history of witchcraft activity and bizarre secret societies, like the Hellfire Club.

As early as 1988 it was being claimed that every year 4,000 children were being sacrificed in satanic rituals across Britain. On a population basis that would have implied that around twenty children from the Glasgow area were being killed as part of an organised network. But was there a factual basis to such claims? The evidence came from alleged confessions from children south of the border and in the USA. It was claimed that children were being forced to take part in bizarre and obscene rituals by Satan worshippers. Animals were ritualistically killed. Babies were murdered and being bred for killing. Cannibalism was practised and naked women used as altars. It was alleged that at one ritual mass a wax model of a businessman was stabbed with a knife over the naked body of a young woman. The model had been filled with animal blood, which gushed out over her body. In its use of a wax effigy it reminded people of the Maxwell case of some three hundred years earlier. It was also claimed that prominent individuals were involved including police chiefs, MPs, judges and councillors. Their position in society meant that they could keep a lid on their secretive cult.

But is Glasgow really a focus for a satanic cult? The jury is out on the matter. Individuals have claimed to be survivors of such a cult, but substantial evidence is lacking. It has even been suggested that false accusations of witchcraft and Satanism is just what the real Satan worshippers want. The sudden emergence of events in Orkney and their collapse in the light of the evidence took the heat off the big centres and led people to doubt if the 'satanic conspiracy' was anything more than the product of vivid imaginations.

And yet: is it all smoke and no fire? Was it pure coincidence that at the very same time that claims of growing satanic influence were being made, pets were disappearing in large numbers? So much so that warnings were being issued to owners to keep an eye on their animals. In a single week at least eight dogs and three cats were reported missing. A spokesman for one animal-welfare organisation warned the public, 'These animals don't go missing for nothing. There must be something behind it.' That 'something', it is alleged, is witchcraft and black magic. It is believed that certain groups do use animals in sickening witchcraft rituals. Parts of horses are particularly prized as these animals have long been seen as having a special link with the worlds beyond. But dogs too have strong associations with the gods from a pagan past. Anubis, the ancient Egyptian god associated with death, is represented with a dog or jackal-like face. There is also the cat goddess Bast, a symbol of the sun. Practitioners of Wicca reject claims that witchcraft is linked to animal sacrifice. That is no doubt true in most cases, but there are always groups on the fringes of any belief ready to go one step further.

Take the apparently motiveless attacks on horses that have puzzled observers for decades. In August 1994 a two-year-old gelding on an Uddingston farm was hit on the head with a claw hammer. A year or so earlier stables at the same place were targeted. A mystery attacker hacked off the tails of two tethered horses. In other attacks a horse was knifed and left bleeding from an eight-inch wound. A similar attack had taken place a few months before. Soon after, a horse was shot in the head and a second animal suffered a bullet wound in the flank. This was part of a pattern of activity that stretched across Scotland. At the same time there were reports of cattle and sheep being mutilated.

There is no doubt that the horse was regarded as a sacred animal. It's claimed that aspiring wizards used to copulate with horses to increase the power of a magic spell, as the seventeenth-century witch, John Weir, confessed. Each part of a horse's body has a special meaning for those who believe in ritual magic. It may be that, by attacking a particular part of the horse, paranormal forces are released, such as the genitalia for sexuality. A horse's tail was also believed to be a powerful medical cure, as was its blood. Wiccans deny any involvement in attacks on animals and it certainly seems that such activities would go against mainstream Wicca creed. In the 1990s a leading Scottish pagan, Dougie, told me: 'Horses are involved in pagan worship, but pagans have nothing to do with these attacks.'

During this period a goat's skull with other objects was found in Sighthill cemetery. It was claimed that a dozen people, some in strange costumes, had been seen dancing in a circle the night before. Whoever was involved, weird incidents continued to occur. As the twenty-first century approached a Glasgow wood carver claimed that he'd been asked to make a variety of strange objects, which could have been used in black magic. An article in the *Evening Times* on 21 February 1998 reported that, 'Satanists have been inundating a Glasgow wood carver with bizarre requests for black magic objects'. These included voodoo tablets and a lifelike wooden carving of a man. The effigy could be used, just like the clay figures of the past, for a psychic assault that would harm an intended target either mentally or physically. A church official reported that, at the same time, he'd received an anguished call from a woman who had become friendly with people who, it turned out, were involved in witchcraft rituals.

So is witchcraft as harmless as is claimed? In the 1990s a leading Glasgow Wiccan, Barry, told me, 'In Wicca we believe that spirit guides can and do assist us with all forms of magick, to change someone's mind about something. For example, some person is refusing to sell a house to a Wicca couple who have offered a fair price.' According to Barry the spirit people would work to change the minds of those refusing to sell, provided that those buying were being fair. There's little doubt that, as in the events of the 1690s, this is the same belief that magic ritual through contacting other dimensions can influence events on earth. Barry and those like him would never use 'magick' for anything but beneficial purposes. But others, using less scrupulous spirits, may take the 'dark path'. If spirits or demons can be contacted by anyone who uses the correct ritual then who can be sure of the way in which this power to control entities from 'other worlds' is put? Are any of us safe from these 'dark forces' who seem willing to put themselves under human control?

# 7

# UFOs

In March 1998 an enormous, unidentified flying object was reported travelling across the Cardonald district of the city. Witnesses described it as 'large and spherical' and watched in amazement as it suddenly stopped moving then just 'hovered in the sky'. The UFO looked as if it had a hollow centre around which pulsated rings of blue, red, green and white lights. A witness to the event remembers it 'flashing very bright colours' and tilting to and fro, until it eventually disappeared behind clouds. One observer at first mistook it for a police helicopter till it rose in the sky and he could see the multi-coloured lights. He watched it shoot off 'at a tremendous speed' aware that he had witnessed 'something inexplicable'. Strange objects of unknown origin moving unchallenged over Scotland's largest city? Is it any wonder people ask just what is going on? The UFO phenomenon is an unsolved mystery that has puzzled observers for decades. Are we being visited by aliens? Is there really a conspiracy to hide the truth about UFOs from the public?

Since UFO sightings first gained worldwide attention following Kenneth Arnold's encounter with disc-shaped objects in the USA in June 1947, UFO reports have been a constant feature of haunted Glasgow. Several of Scotland's earliest UFO encounters emerged from the city. One afternoon in 1952 Joan Torrance was leaving Elder Park primary school with her friends. It was around four and, as she crossed the playground, she became aware of a dark shadow falling across the school. Joan looked up and saw something she never forgot. About a hundred feet overhead there hung a sombrero-shaped object, tilted slightly on its axis. It seemed to be rotating. Then, suddenly, as if aware it was being watched, the UFO shot off across the city emitting a strange whirring sound. This wasn't the imagination of a child. The UFO was seen by several adults as it crossed Glasgow.

It was almost certainly the same object seen by George Byng, among others, as he also observed it close to four o'clock. George was fifteen and a third-year pupil at Greenock High. He was not alone in his sighting, other pupils and teachers also witnessed the UFO. George described it as a 'circular, shining, copper object' that 'appeared above the hills, travelling in a straight line and at a steady speed of perhaps 100 miles per hour and at a height of about 1,500 to 2,000 feet'. One difference from Joan Torrance's experience was that, according to George, 'It was absolutely soundless.' But George was further away from the object and so, like a distant aircraft, the UFO might have been too far off to catch any noise. The object headed out in a north-easterly direction.

Some residents of the city believe that their UFO experiences were spiritual in nature. In May 1976 Allistair MacNeil was sitting in a flat in Westbourne Gardens, in Glasgow's affluent West End, with two friends. Allistair glanced at the clock, noting that it was three in the morning, and thinking that he had been chatting for several hours. At that very moment, through the window, he caught a glimpse of something moving. Looking outside he saw a large, silver-coloured, disc-shaped object hovering about one hundred feet above an open, grass-covered space, directly opposite the flat. Allistair judged the 'craft' to be about sixty-feet across, with porthole-type windows visible around the upper section. As he and his friends watched the disc suddenly came hurtling towards them then abruptly shot skywards soaring above the rooftops. The incident had a dramatic effect on Allistair who felt that the object had emitted a strange aura of almost 'divine' proportions.

Allistair is by no means alone in feeling that he had experienced an event of life-changing proportions. Arthur Govan also felt that his experience had altered his view of the world. Arthur was driving on the A82 towards Dumbarton, and, around 2 p.m., approached the traffic lights at Dalreoch junction. At this point he was 'assailed by a powerful, sparkling light that had no obvious source'. He knew it could not be the sun, as he could see it clearly to the south-east, but the light was so strong that Arthur felt he was going to be blinded. He reported that, 'the light flowed in a shallow ribbon over the hill of an old quarry to my right, the south-west. It was of a different quality from sunlight, almost pure white and sparkling, as if consisting of thousands of little stars.' To Arthur it flowed like a river. Whatever the source of the light it affected Arthur's attitude to life, bringing a 'vast reduction in materialistic attitudes'. It awakened in him, he said, 'a spiritual awareness' that gradually transformed his life.

Though the link between 'nuts and bolts' UFOs and a spiritual experience does not, at first glance, appear obvious, it is explicit in the experience of one witness, an experience that raises a host of questions about the UFO phenomenon. Could we really be in contact with God's messengers? Are UFOs the modern equivalent of angels? In 1971 Eleanor Harvey was living in Cumnock Road, opposite King's Park. 'It was a beautiful early July morning', she recalled, 'and I was waiting my turn to get into the bathroom.' As she stood patiently she glanced out of the window. It was a normal rush hour, with heavy traffic and people standing at the bus stop. Then 'all of a sudden I heard a noise. It sounded as if something had landed on the roof.' Eleanor thought it might be workmen sorting her neighbour's television aerial, although, as it was eight o'clock, it seemed rather early to start the job. Her surprise deepened when she heard 'what sounded like the engine of a small aircraft being switched off', followed rapidly 'by a broad stream of light', which came shining straight through the window. The beam struck Eleanor on her forehead just above her eyes.

Surprised, Eleanor drew back from the window, and then heard a shout. A face appeared, 'beautiful and sad'. The beam was shining through the image, but Eleanor could make out 'silver hair . . . cut to shoulder length, a moustache and a neat, square-cut beard'. The eyes were brown, a shade of hazel. The mysterious entity looked at Eleanor and she felt 'as if it was stripping my very soul' even though 'no words were spoken'. By this point Eleanor must have been able to see more of the being, as she noted that he raised his right hand with his palm towards her in what she interpreted as a 'sign of peace'. As she watched the image grew stronger, so that eventually she could see all of him. He was dressed in a long gown that shone gold in the still-present beam of light but which she judged, in reality, to be coloured white. She noted one odd fact about the gown. There were no obvious joins or seams even though it covered his entire body to his ankles. On his feet were leather sandals and around his waist, loosely slung, a gold cord, knotted, which almost reached the floor. The spell was broken by a scratching sound, followed by a noise like a motor being started. Then came the rattle on the roof 'and the invisible machine took off', as Eleanor put it. She rushed to the window, but couldn't see anything. Then a voice said, 'I am the light of the world. He that believeth in me shall have everlasting life.' Eleanor believed she had been visited by Jesus Christ. Curiously, and though Eleanor did not appear to be aware of it, the phrase 'light of the world' is used in the Bible specifically to denote Jesus, and salvation is defined as 'walking in his light' and being enlightened by it. In ancient belief light was holy and the scriptures associated it with God. UFOs and the Bible? An unlikely connection. But there have been experiences elsewhere in which witnesses have reported angels and alien spacecraft appearing together. Other encounters, on the other hand, suggest that these experiences can be far from spiritual.

Eleanor's encounter wasn't the first time Scotland had been visited by an alien entity. And one of a different kind. In 1955 a strange event occurred in Belhaven Terrace which is, incidentally, right beside Westbourne Gardens where Allistair MacNeil would later undergo his 1976 encounter. Local children regularly played there on a bit of waste ground, which at the time was overgrown with trees and shrubs. Eight-year-old Emma Roberts was cooking potatoes over a small fire in this spot with some friends when she suddenly became aware of being watched by what she would later describe as strange 'beings' or entities. Emma's sister was terrified by the appearance of these strangers and immediately ran home. Emma, however, was fascinated. She carried on looking at them, noticing that the first two entities had now been joined by several others. The group seemed to be focusing their attention on the ground and Emma realised that they were all hovering a little above the earth rather than standing on it. All the beings looked exactly the same: tall, thin, very pale-skinned, wearing long, floating white garments with white caps. They had distinctly pointed faces with deep and penetrating eyes. Then, as if a spell had been broken, the entities seemed to 'switch on' to Emma's presence and turned in her direction, looking directly at her. The first being then started moving towards her, followed by the others. For the first time Emma felt frightened and turned and ran till she reached the safety of her home. As far as she is aware the entities made no attempt to enter the house.

An intriguing aspect of Glasgow's UFO phenomenon is the sheer range of incidents reported. But it should be remembered that most UFO sightings do not involve a 'close encounter', either of a 'spacecraft' or of an alien entity. The vast majority of UFOs reported consist of strange-looking lights or an unusual configuration of lights that are moving around the sky in an odd way. Sometimes the lights will come closer and the witness will catch sight of a solid object, not necessarily of the disc variety, as 'UFOs' come in all shapes and sizes. Are these sightings evidence of alien intelligence in the skies above us? Is there some plan behind this activity or are they simply random encounters? Or could there be something more sinister going on? Are we under some kind of observation? Perhaps the incidents themselves can give us a clue.

In July 1966 a 'large, white and circular' object was seen by several people at Anniesland Cross. Patrick Connelly claimed, 'It looked very much like a classic flying saucer. It speeded up gradually and climbed away at a distance.' Another witness, Chris, reported, 'I got a clear view . . . it was no trick of the light.' Glasgow weather centre suggested that it could have been an optical illusion caused by sunlight shining on a large aircraft. However, be that as it may, air-traffic control confirmed that there were no aircraft in the area at the time. So just what did the witnesses glimpse?

Ten years later, on 5 October 1976, Ben Goodwin, at the time a serving policeman, a recent recruit to the Strathclyde force, watched a mysterious silver ball descend on the city. Ben, who was in Drumchapel when the incident occurred, noted that the time was 9.40 p.m. and that the object seemed to be coming down to the left of Glasgow airport. As the glowing ball reached the ground it swung back and forth like a pendulum then suddenly shot skywards and disappeared.

Amazingly, over twenty years after Ben's sighting, a similar object was spotted over the west of the city. On 17 January 1999, at around two in the afternoon, an unidentified flying object was seen as two civilian aircraft flew by. The UFO was oval in shape and appeared a brilliant white. It blinked at regular intervals, which could have been due to the object moving from side to side as it sped across the sky. The object rapidly passed the two aircraft. A witness estimated it was travelling at a speed between 1,000 and 1,800 miles per hour. Fast, but nowhere near the rate reported by the witness of a UFO in 1984.

The witness, who does not wish to be identified, was an amateur pilot at the time and so well used to watching the skies. On this occasion he was working on the upper floors of a tall office block in the city centre. It was a clear day and he was mentally clocking landmarks well known to pilots. As he glanced towards Eaglesham he caught sight of a 'multi-coloured pink, silver and grey craft', which was cigar shaped. It moved at fantastic speed across his line of vision. Using his experience as a pilot and his knowledge of the area he calculated that it covered a distance of twenty-five miles in two seconds, a speed of 45,000 miles per hour. If most UFOs are travelling at similar speeds it may explain why they are not often seen and rarely tracked on radar. It may well be that reported UFOs are simply a tiny fraction of the total number of objects intruding on our space. We may be seeing only those that are slow moving, or that stand out for some other reason, such as the enormous UFO over a mile long reported over Bellahouston park. If these truly are nuts-and-bolts craft from distant galaxies then there is no reason why these objects should be exclusively large or small. Like craft used for travelling on our own planet they could be of various sizes, depending upon their use.

The range of reports from individuals is evidence that 'something' odd is going on in the skies above. But can we get closer for a clearer view? Most sightings are by one person, a single witness, but sightings by several witnesses are less frequent. They suggest that the phenomenon is genuine, though we may interpret it in different ways. On Wednesday, 4 February 1996 David, a civil servant, witnessed a UFO as he left the Kelvin Hall. He reported that the object was 'bright white and looked some way off, but it was moving at some rate of knots'. David said that it reminded him of pictures he had seen of an object re-entering earth's atmosphere. In fact hundreds of witnesses in Glasgow at this time saw a strange object move across the sky. The UFO was travelling at a phenomenal speed trailing an orange flame in its wake. At one point it appeared to hang motionless in the sky for several minutes before shooting away again. Meanwhile CB enthusiasts noticed that the UFO was creating a loud buzzing sound on their radios and causing the needle on the dial to jerk rapidly. Having passed over the city the UFO appeared to crash land some distance away, on the island of Jura. It exploded in a ball of flame. The authorities claimed that this was simply a 'forest fire', but it seemed too much of a coincidence to be explained away so simply. From the various accounts of the event it appears that an object of some kind hit the ground. So if this was simply a piece of space debris, as was suggested, why all the secrecy? The event has never been satisfactorily explained and the authorities continue to deny the evidence that something inexplicable occurred that day.

Mass sightings of a UFO are unusual. Similarly, most UFO witnesses experience a single encounter, but some people have several. Rita from Maryhill experienced her first UFO in 1968. She observed a cigar-shaped object, which was silvery-grey. Then in October 1997 she saw a disc-shaped UFO with a structure like a raised cabin on top. The object was travelling at high speed and around the disc were dark areas that could have been windows. The UFO was enveloped by a shimmering heat haze, which might be evidence of a propulsion system at work. The disc was being followed by four small objects which, to Rita, also appeared to be disc-shaped. Witnesses have reported elsewhere the sighting of a 'mother' ship, which then sends out unmanned probes. Other encounters reported by Rita include strange lights of different colours moving at fantastic speeds. But the strangest sighting was that of an elongated, worm-like structure, red and white in colour, jumping about the sky and glowing like a fluorescent light. It could also be described as serpent-shaped and, if seen in the skies in ancient times, might explain why serpent worship or its opposite, deep suspicion of this creature, was so much a part of ancient belief, as evidenced in the Bible in connection with Adam and Eve in the garden of Eden.

Some experiences can be intense and personal, involve several witnesses and many sightings. In an amazing personal document, entitled *The Eleventh Hour*, James Welsh records the bizarre events he experienced in December 1999 as the millennium approached. It all started early on the morning of Saturday, 4 December: as James was returning home to Newlands in the south of Glasgow after a night's dancing at a club in the Arches he spotted a strange object. It was a light in the sky, due south, which flashed from green to red then to blue and finally began to glow with an intense, white light. It then abruptly shot up at forty-five degrees, at high speed, leaving behind a trail of white light then, as suddenly, returned to its original position. The object next performed a series of abrupt forty-five degree turns, getting ever faster as it did so. A circle of white light formed at the same time as the object disappeared behind it. Then, in an instant, it pulled out of the spin and moved off to James's left at tremendous speed. All of this was also witnessed by a friend, who had been chatting with him at the time. James raced home and alerted his brother, who went outside with him to observe the UFO. James described the light coming from the object as 'intense'. It appeared closer now and James could make out a diamond shape. He also noted that the coloured lights were being projected from the centre of the 'diamond', which began to glow. A brilliant white spread over the whole object, and then suddenly stopped. The next moment the object had vanished. At exactly 4.45 a.m.

James rang the police at East Kilbride as he thought the UFO was heading in that direction and also spoke to police in Rutherglen, but was told that no one else had reported a sighting. It should be added that the role of the constabulary in relation to UFO reports is unclear. There is some evidence that the police, on occasion, forward UFO reports to a central location. However, some forces deny that they even log reports. Retired officers have informed me that UFOs are regularly reported, often by police on patrol, but they are ignored. It is easy to see a conspiracy in all of this, but it may be a conspiracy of ignorance as opposed to anything more sinister. In any case the police may have chosen to ignore the events, but James couldn't. Whatever James had seen it had certainly focused his mind. The following day he booked a trip to the Egyptian city of Luxor. This was certainly an appropriate destination. It has long been suspected that the ancient Egyptians knew a great deal more about the universe than we have been led to believe and may even have been in touch with civilisations on other planets. The alleged existence of pyramids on Mars though, of course, highly controversial has been cited as an obvious link. There have been many reports of pyramid-shaped UFOs and, it is argued, this explains why identical structures were erected by the Egyptians: that is, as a 'sign' to space travellers. Another suggestion is the pyramids functioned as a machine that generated an unknown power, which allowed the Egyptians to contact entities from other worlds. A trip to Egypt can open your mind to a range of amazing possibilities. Did the ancients, as some suggest, originate in a far-off planet and colonise earth?

Perhaps James was experiencing, for the first time, just a little bit of what the ancient Egyptians had taken for granted. But the events of 4 December were only the beginning of an astonishing series of incidents. On Friday, 10 December James was heading for Mount Florida to meet a friend. As he took a short cut through the station and climbed the stairs James glimpsed a bright light passing the buildings in front of him. The sighting was over in a second, but James was intrigued and ran to Cathcart Road where he caught sight of the object again. James wanted to get a second opinion so drew the object to the attention of a passer-by. The UFO disappeared, but another object appeared. It was flashing in a way reminiscent of his sighting the previous Saturday. He estimated it was between eight thousand and twelve thousand feet up, and heading south. The object then started to behave in a strange way, shooting rapidly across the sky. James moved into a lane to get away from the glare of the street lights, but the object began to fade and then disappeared. He checked his watch. It was 4.45 p.m. The fact that his previous sighting had also taken place at 4.45, though in the morning, struck him as odd.

The next day, Saturday, 11 December, James had further sightings. That day he went with a friend to the Virgin Megastore. The band Travis were giving a free concert. The lead singer, Fran Healy, had been in James's class at secondary school so he was particularly keen to secure a ticket. He was planning to head into town to get in the queue early so it was at 4.45 a.m. – that sequence of numbers again – that he stepped through his front door into a very cold night. As James puts it, 'the weird stuff started again'. This time it was a strange, flashing, white object, which suddenly seemed to explode in a blaze of light across the sky. James notes that the 'blast of blinding light . . . illuminated a large portion of the sky around it'. In fact, he and a relative had spotted two UFOs at this time, which seemed to be flashing signals to each other. James claims, 'It was as if there was a giant camera in the sky that photographed us, and, when this went off, light seemed to bounce in every direction within the light itself.' He headed to Queen's Park recreation ground where he and a relative saw many UFOs that morning. He describes 'countless sightings of objects at high altitudes . . . moving fast, stopping and turning at sharp angles, leaving trails of light behind them'. At other times UFOs would 'flash out light pulses to one another'. James is of the opinion that the objects might be 'conducting a scan of the area around Rutherglen' as they 'were moving across the sky from left to right, going over the same area again and again'.

Suddenly, one of the craft dropped behind flats at Toryglen. The object was glowing white and about the length of the building, which James judged to be about 150 feet. The UFO had given out a trail of light as it descended and as 'the UFO disappeared from sight . . . the trail of light also began to vanish. As the light came down to the top of the building and was about to fade from sight the UFO rose up again and the light trail came down to touch it.' The UFO then shot off, leaving a stream of light in its wake. James notes that 'as the sun began to rise in the east the UFOs departed in this direction as the clouds closed in' then 'three RAF aircraft jetted overhead in the direction of the departing UFOs. The three jets flew in a triangle formation, with their jet streams on.' It was now 6.45. They had been watching the UFOs for two hours.

It goes without saying that the military usually deny any interest in UFOs unless they are seen as a threat to national security. Witness evidence and documentation released under the Freedom of

Information Act suggest more interest in these reports than they are willing to admit.

On Tuesday, 14 December James had another experience, which he describes as 'one of the most significant events in my life'. It began when, glancing through the hall window, he spotted a flashing UFO. The object 'performed a skipping motion where it jumped to a higher position without moving'. James was getting a lift from his dad into the city centre, where he worked, and on the way he spotted the UFO again although it kept disappearing from view. As they approached the bridge over the river James saw a police helicopter 'flying low over the Clyde'. He guessed that the police 'were airborne in response to the presence of the UFO'. As James got out of his dad's car, aware of the noise of the rotors, he noticed that the helicopter 'was just above a building over Argyle Street'. It was now 7.52 p.m. and James was still watching the sky when his attention was caught by something at great altitude', which was 'pulsating sharp bursts of light'. James then received a real shock, which he said 'nothing could have prepared me for':

My gaze had just fixed upon the flashing light and my vision focused on it when the sky directly above my head suddenly vanished and became pure white. It only lasted for a split second before it was gone and the sky returned again. As I looked up towards the flashing UFO the buildings on either side of me provided a frame of reference as I looked skywards. Now something passed directly over the buildings above my head, from the north travelling south, at an incredible speed. The sky became pure white as it passed directly over my head.

The UFO left behind an enormous line of white light that spread across the sky for a brief second before it began to disappear. As the object had been moving very rapidly, James could not be sure of its shape, but as he had seen it against a backdrop of buildings he judged it to be twice their size and the trail of light about 150-feet across. The police helicopter by comparison was like 'a dragonfly and was dwarfed by the UFO'.

This incident had a tremendous impact on James. In *The Eleventh Hour* he writes: 'At that moment I became more aware of my own existence than I've ever been.' He was so convinced of the reality of the event that once he'd finished his shift and returned home he rang Glasgow airport and made an official UFO report.

But this dramatic event was not James's last sighting. Scouring the skies from the football pitches beside the Queen's Park, James and a relative saw a glowing, white UFO shooting towards the ground at an angle of forty-five degrees leaving a trail of white light behind. As it approached the ground it reduced speed, changed direction and descended straight down, appearing to drop behind the high flats in Mount Florida. They then spotted through the trees a glowing, orange ball in the distance. It rose slowly and seemed to wobble. They spotted a second glowing object over Glasgow airport. It should be mentioned that the airport seems to attract a lot of UFO attention with objects reported travelling from the direction of the Camspsie hills and appearing to zigzag over it as if recording activities. Around 5.30 a.m. James observed a triangular formation of RAF planes, probably Tornados, shoot overhead. Had this been in response to the appearance of the UFOs?

This was James's last sighting. When he returned from his trip to Egypt James found a response from the Ministry of Defence waiting for him:

> Their response was as unbelievable as this story. According to them there was nothing of defence interest and nothing was tracked on radar etc . . . the letter made me feel that they were trying to tell me that the incidents that I witnessed simply did not happen and that I was wrong to assume that we were being visited by aliens because the MOD would know about it if they did. In short, I witnessed something that didn't happen. I knew better.

What can we make of James's sightings? Why was there such a burst of activity? It may be that somehow James had 'opened up' to the possibility of alien life forms and whatever is out there responded. This might explain why people who were with him also experienced the phenomena.

Occasionally, a sighting can be so strange as to leave you puzzling as to exactly what we are dealing with. On 15 December 1983 Tom Coventry left for work at 6.25 a.m., following his usual route down Menock Road in the King's Park area towards the bus stop, where he waited for the bus to arrive. The weather was crisp and dry, with good visibility. As he stood at the stop his attention was caught by an object in the distance, low down and heading in his direction. Tom, at first, took it to be a plane of some kind. He then noticed that flame was spurting from the rear and the thought crossed his mind that it was in trouble. But as it got closer he realised that it wasn't a plane at all. Around him things went silent as if he had entered another world. The object he had been watching was now right over him and hovered a mere twenty feet away. Tom had never seen anything like it. 'It was coloured grey,' he recalls, 'shaped like a railway carriage, but with a curved roof.' The craft made a crackling and humming noise, which reminded Tom of electricity. He could make out three porthole-shaped windows at the front and through them he glimpsed an interior that seemed to be swirling with yellow smoke. The object moved slowly off in the direction of a nearby railway bridge, where it stopped for a split second before shooting skywards vertically then travelling across the city. What struck Tom as particularly strange was that no one else, not even passengers on a bus passing beneath the bridge, had noticed the object. He also remarked that, 'one of the strangest parts was when the object did start moving, noise from all around started up again'. It was as if it all rushed back!'

One singularly odd aspect of Tom's sighting was the fire he saw coming from the UFO. It is hard to believe that a futuristic spacecraft would use a propulsion system like those on earth today.

Everyone would accept that to cover vast distances a completely new method of travel has to be discovered. It is interesting to note, however, that in the 1990s Catherine McEwan from Pollokshields, along with another witness, saw a strange object moving across the sky. Unlike Tom's it was round and shining, but like the UFO seen by Tom it was spurting flame and looked as if it was on fire. Similar sightings have been reported right across the country. It does make you wonder if we are connecting with other dimensions rather than being visited by beings from distant planets. Had Tom, in fact, 'tuned in' to another dimension for a few moments? The strange sensation he experienced, and the sudden quiet that abruptly ended when the UFO disappeared, might suggest this was the case. Or was this UFO monitoring Tom? A clue might be provided by a sighting at Alexandria. On 25 October 1996, at 4.20 p.m., a witness looking out from the back window of his house in Buchan Avenue with others observed two objects like football floodlights, floating and chasing each other. One seemed to survey a telegraph pole then hovered over a sheep. Both UFOs were silver coloured. The witness got a good view of the objects as he watched them through a telescope.

Were these UFOs unmanned droids sent to collect information? Other witnesses have reported similar encounters. In 1967 Bill McDougall, walking beside George Square, was shocked when a round object about the size of a football shot past him. As it went by he could hear a high-pitched, hissing noise. It left behind a strong smell of sulphur. But the surprising part of the event to Bill was that the UFO appeared to be under some kind of intelligent control and gave the impression of moving with a clear purpose.

It is interesting to note that George Square has attracted other UFO attention. Thirty years after Bill McDougall's encounter a couple crossing the east side of the square saw an octagonal-shaped UFO, about thirty-feet wide, hovering overhead. The bizarre aspect of the sighting was that no one else seemed aware of the object. It vanished in an instant in a flash of blue light. Blue, of course, in many parts of Scotland, is an indication of 'other worldly' phenomena, from the blue men of the Minch to the small blue men seen in the woods of Meigle in the 1960s. Could there be a common pattern in all this?

It may well be there is no pattern simply because UFO incidents are so varied. But while that may be true there is evidence that links the typical 'lights in the sky' UFO report to 'close encounters' and interaction with individual witnesses. In the 1990s, in the East End of the city, James Montgomery and his friend Jane set out at five to eleven one night to buy a takeaway. They noticed a light travelling across the sky. After leaving the fast-food outlet carrying their meals they headed home and, as they did so, saw the light again. Nothing else seems to have occurred that they were consciously aware of. However, when they got home their daughter asked them where on earth they had got to as they had been away for so long. Though, at first, James couldn't make sense of what his daughter was asking, when he unwrapped his 'hot' meal he found that it was stone cold. 'Frozen', to use James's terminology, and inedible.

It turned out that forty-five minutes of the couple's journey could not be accounted for; a classic, missing-time event. The take-away was only a few minutes away so, clearly, there must have been a considerable delay between the time the food was purchased and James reaching home. What had happened during those lost minutes? In Scotland's other famous missing-time case, the encounter of Gary Woods and Colin Wright on the A70 in August 1992, the events that occurred during the lost hour after they encountered a shining light over the road only emerged after they underwent hypnotic regression. They had been abducted, probably by aliens. It was not considered appropriate to use hypnosis in James's case, so we may never learn just what happened though the use of regression hypnosis is a controversial area and its reliability often questioned. James, however, experienced a second, even more dramatic, encounter.

He and Jane were walking home after a night at the cinema. They noticed a light travelling across the sky, which suddenly moved down and towards them. They started walking a little faster, but the object seemed to be getting ever closer. James was unnerved. The street was unusually deserted and it seemed unnaturally quiet. The couple started to run and fully expected to encounter the 'light' as they rounded a corner, but, in fact, the UFO rose into the sky where it was joined by a second. Both lights then headed in the direction of Coatbridge. James told me:

> What I found strange was that there was no one about. No cars. No people. No one. I would have expected to see people. It came down to within ninety feet of us. It looked like a yellow orb. There was a strange feeling in the area. It felt as if there was a vacuum round about us. The UFO went behind a house. Then came back and met up with another one and then shot off.

There seems no obvious explanation as to why James and those close to him should become the focus of such attention. But he was certainly convinced that, for some reason, the UFO was attempting to interact with them.

At least Jane and James lived to tell the tale. On Christmas Eve 1975, fifty-five-year-old Glasgow-based Peter Gibbs, a former leader of the Scottish Symphony Orchestra, was combining business and pleasure on the island of Mull. Gibbs was the managing director of Gibbs & Rae, a company he had established three years before, which owned and developed property in the Glasgow area. Gibbs was looking for fresh challenges and was considering buying on the island. He used the Glen Forsa hotel, located near the village of Salen, as his base. Whether by choice or accident he had booked into the only hotel on the island with a landing strip in its grounds. Shortly after arriving Gibbs hired a Cessna and travelled to Oban where he picked it up and flew it back to the Glen Forsa landing strip. He passed the next few hours relaxing over drinks and dinner at the hotel.

After dinner Gibbs announced that he intended to make a night-time flight. He didn't explain why it had suddenly become urgent or why it had to be carried out on a landing area that had no proper lighting system. The airstrip was essentially a flattened area of grass, which would have been very difficult to spot in the dark even by the most experienced pilot. Gibbs's strange solution was to have two ordinary torches put on the ground as landing beacons, an arrangement later described by an aviation expert as 'absolutely worthless as a form of indication'. Ignoring the obvious danger Gibbs took off in the Cessna around 9.30 p.m., made a circuit of the hotel then disappeared from view behind a clump of trees. The plane did not reappear, although there was no sound of a crash or even a flare from an explosion. By ten, with no further sighting of the Cessna, it was clear that something had gone awry though it was possible that Gibbs, realising the hazard of a night landing, had headed to a better-equipped strip in Glasgow. At half-past ten the hotel contacted Prestwick air traffic control. Police arrived and within a short time had established that no plane had landed at any local airstrip. Gibbs seemed to have vanished into the night.

As Christmas Day dawned teams combed the island interior and the coast looking for the Cessna. By the twenty-ninth, after an exhaustive search, it seemed that Gibbs was not going to be easily found and efforts were scaled down. And a puzzle it remained until 21 April 1976, a full four months after Gibbs and the Cessna had disappeared. A local shepherd caught sight of an object balanced on a fallen tree trunk. It turned out to be a body of a man, quite dead, lying on its back with the legs stretched out on either side of the trunk and the head resting gently on the ground.

It was the corpse of Peter Gibbs, which had turned up less than a mile from the Glen Forsa hotel in a place that had not only been thoroughly searched, but also had been passed at regular intervals by the shepherd who eventually discovered the body. He was sure that it had not been there previously. Another strange fact was the absence of bone fractures or impact marks, which would have been the inevitable result if either the Cessna had crashed or Gibbs had tried to jump out. He was not even wearing a parachute.

So how had Gibbs arrived there? He did not appear to have spent time in the sea as there was no salt on his clothes. Even if he had managed to bring the plane down to stalling speed and jumped out he could hardly have avoided an injury of some kind. And the pathologist reported that there was not the slightest evidence of any such injury. In any event, could Gibbs or any pilot flying over countryside in pitch darkness, have brought a plane down to a height from which he could eject safely? And if he had, where was the Cessna?

It was to be another twelve years before the plane was discovered, lying about three hundred yards offshore, at the entrance to Fishnish Bay in the Sound of Mull. But that only deepened the puzzle. The aircraft had definitely crashed, but how had Gibbs managed to abandon it, swim ashore and then climb a hill only to die of exposure. To get to that spot he had to cross a main road so why not do the obvious thing and wait to flag down help? It all made little sense. The fatal-accident inquiry held in Oban in June 1976 did not reveal anything new, although, in the aftermath, one strange fact emerged. At the moment of Gibbs's disappearance, close to the spot where the Cessna was later discovered, a strange series of unidentified lights had been seen in the night sky. In fact the area where Gibbs vanished has a long tradition of unexplained lights, known in the past as 'fairy lights', though today we would classify them as UFOs. Could the sightings of these lights explain why Gibbs's Cessna ended up in the water when the plane was last reported heading inland and away from the sea?

Might this, in fact, be a case of alien abduction, with Peter Gibbs removed from his plane by extraterrestrials then weeks after returned to a Mull hillside? In the United States just a few weeks after Gibbs's disappearance, forestry worker Travis Walton was taken aboard a strange craft and days later dumped on a roadside in a state of shock. His account is controversial, but it does bear similarities to the Gibbs incident. Could there really be some unknown vortex of power that can swallow people, but for some reason disgorged Peter Gibbs on a lonely hillside? The experience of James Montgomery in the East End suggests that behind those unexplained lights in the night sky, there lies a much less reassuring phenomenon. One that can have fatal consequences for humans.

Sceptics, of course, in spite of vast numbers of sightings, continue to downplay the phenomenon, which, according to them, is either the result of an over-vivid imagination or simply a case of mistaken identity. Fortunately, we can add photographic evidence to sightings by individuals. Does this prove the reality of UFOs? In June 2001 I was contacted by professional photographer Mark Rannules, who had taken some astonishing pictures of a UFO. Mark had been snapping a few frames from his flat at Broomhill Drive in the West End at 4.30 a.m. looking towards the high flats at Kelvindale and the Campsie Hills. It wasn't until he developed his pictures that he realised he had captured an amazing UFO image. The object, a photograph of which appeared in the *Daily Record*, looked clearly disc-shaped, like a 'traditional flying saucer' of 1940s vintage. The images caught just after showed a green, glowing object. It is possible the UFO had 'fired up' as it prepared either to enter another dimension or to shoot off at amazing speed. Interestingly, a witness, Martin, had reported seeing a UFO in the same place six days earlier. He was watching meteors over the Campsies at 4.30 a.m. and said, 'What appeared to be a star grew to about twenty-five times its original size. The flash of light was incredibly bright and I know for sure it wasn't an aeroplane.' A second witness also caught a glimpse at around the same time. He had seen 'a thin streak of light in the direction of the Campsies. It was reddish in colour and was there one minute and gone the next.'

In the 1980s, a photo was taken over Clydeside docks. When developed a glowing, disc-like object appeared on the photo, which the witness had not been aware of at the time. Analysis of the snap revealed that the camera had definitely caught something solid. It was not a trick of the light or a technical fault of the lens or film. However, it was not possible to make out any features, other than the fact that it was spherical and glowing. Why wasn't the object captured on film visible to the naked eye? According to some theories UFOs can make themselves invisible by locating in a section of the light spectrum that is not normally visible to the human eye, in the same way that the Stealth bomber makes itself invisible to radar. It's a huge step up in terms of technology, but not, in theory, impossible. It is interesting to note that in 1957 John Anderson from Dennistoun was travelling close to Govan docks on the top deck of a tram when he spotted two strange objects. In appearance they looked 'perfectly round and glistened like silver'. Evidence for the view, argued by a number of ufologists, that we are being monitored by alien life forms who are, in addition, particularly interested in areas of industrial activity.

But have aliens already landed in Glasgow and are the authorities working with them? Events in John McReady's life have convinced him that they are. John was a straightforward, easygoing individual till he had a UFO experience and then his world rapidly fell apart. In September 1973 he saw the shining craft – which had a broad, red band encircling it – from the deck of the ship he was working on in the North Sea. This started a train of events that was to reach a climax in his native city of Glasgow. The problems started almost immediately after his sighting. To John the glowing object with a distinct hump-back hovering over the water was as clear as a bell, but others on board either seemed to ignore it or attempted to discredit his sighting. John was taken aback by their attitude. He even began to doubt his own experience though in the back of his mind he knew that what he had seen was all too real. But it began to become an obsession. He could not get the sighting out of his head. He took a job on land, but could not escape the impact of his sighting. It had turned his world upside down. Even more disturbing was the sensation that alien beings were contacting him and then warning him not to discuss his experiences. John was by now becoming quite frightened. His marriage failed and, he readily confesses, he experienced a mental breakdown. But his life had been normal till the UFO came along. Problems had arisen from the trauma of his other-worldly experience. It shattered his normal perception of the world.

Having recovered from his breakdown to the extent that he could go back to work John took a job working in the kitchens of a city-centre hotel. He was getting on well, so well that he confided details of his UFO experiences to Roy, a colleague. John noticed that Roy gave him a strange look. He could have kicked himself for talking about the UFO. He realised he'd made a mistake and vowed not to open his mouth on the subject again. The very next morning John was sacked. Food had been left out overnight that should have been put in the fridge. John was made the scapegoat and told to leave. In his mind there was no doubt that the two events were linked. He had made the mistake of discussing his experience and this was a warning to him to keep quiet.

All in his imagination? Even John was not completely sure, until a later encounter finally convinced him. A few days after he was fired he was returning to his flat and, just as he entered the tenement close, he was grabbed by two men. They were not 'men-in-black'; on the contrary they were dressed in ordinary clothes, but they had an extraordinary message to convey. They warned him not to discuss his experiences. They repeated information, which he previously thought he had either dreamt or imagined. They told him there were aliens on earth and that they had been around for a while. They looked human and you would pass them in the street without a second glance. They had underground bases in various locations, including Scotland. They were telling him this so he would know that it was real and that he must keep quiet.

John was understandably shaken and for ten years was nervous about relating his story. He told me, 'I've already trusted the wrong people and nearly got myself killed.' He truly believes that aliens are already among us. What is striking about John's story is that it was told long before accounts of underground bases and 'aliens among us' were widespread. He later underwent hypnotic regression, but with limited success. It was as if there was a block on his memory. In subsequent years others who have had alien encounters have also claimed that they were taken to underground bases rather than spacecraft in the sky.

So how should we weigh up the evidence? In June 2006 I appeared on BBC Television's *Newsnight* programme with inter-viewer Jeremy Paxton to discuss the UFO issue in relation to top-secret flights over Scotland by technologically advanced US military planes, especially the Aurora. There is no doubt that over Scotland's west coast and down the Clyde there had been, in the 1980s and 1990s, numerous reports of triangular- and pyramid-shaped objects. There was a suggestion that they were advanced US spy planes being flown from Machrihanish and tested over Scotland. Reports of UFOs could have been the result of seeing these craft though, in many cases, the manoeuvrability of the UFOs did not fit in with the capability of even the most advanced aeroplanes. But explaining away UFO sightings as top-secret spy planes was a common theme of the 1990s. In 1995, when, as reported in the *Greenock Telegraph*, Keith McCumiskey videoed a strange object over the Clyde, described as 'bright green and round with three bumps and a silver underside' one of the sugges-tions made was that it could be the Aurora spy plane.

But it's too easy to dismiss the UFO phenomenon as simply a case of mistaken identity. Distant lights in a dark sky may, or may not, be significant. But close-up sightings of disc- or more strangely shaped craft are harder to dismiss, however strange the encounter. On top of that we have photographic evidence and, strangest of all, those who believe their experience suggests aliens may be already among us. Most people would be unwilling to go that far. But most can surely agree that the UFO phenomenon, as experienced over Glasgow's skies, raises many, as yet unanswered, questions.

# 8

# Ritual Murders

Can the forces of the supernatural drive people to kill? Or do people use murder as a means to generate powerful energy for magic? Or could both be true? Even though every aspect of the paranormal has put in an appearance in Glasgow it is still disturbing to note that at least six cases of murder with ritual overtones have been documented within the city's boundaries in the recent past. Why and for what purpose murder should be changed into a ritual is a mystery in itself. Is it simply the product of a twisted mind? Or can we see in this act the work of dark forces? A living evil that takes over the body of a man or woman and then drives them to commit the ultimate crime?

There was nothing obviously bad about Sheena McLaughlan, who was brought up in Maryhill. She did well at school and was bright enough to start a course at an Edinburgh college, though she later dropped out and moved back to Glasgow to live with her mother in Raeberry Street. The truth was that academic study wasn't Sheena's strong point. She had two overriding interests. She desperately wanted to become a pop star and as a teenager had developed an obsession with pop music. She would lock herself in her room where she practised playing the guitar and sang songs she had composed herself. She started her own band, but felt they weren't good enough for her so dropped them and started another band, which also collapsed. There was an aimless quality about Sheena's life. She wanted success, but never knew how to get it.

At the same time, her life was being driven in another direction. She had become immersed in the occult. It began when, as a ten-year-old, she became fascinated with the black-magic novels of writer Dennis Wheatley. She learned about tarot cards and used them to give people readings. It was said that she possessed a natural psychic talent. In her late teens Sheena began having visions in which she saw people, dressed like monks, from other worlds. One, who was particularly forceful, wore yellow robes, and claimed to be the ghost of a long-dead Tibetan guru. It soon became her spirit guide and encouraged her to develop her psychic powers. Sheena was convinced that he had her best interests at heart.

But was there a connection between Sheena's spirit guide and what happened next? When Sheena fell pregnant, at the age of twenty-two, following a trip to London to learn more about the tarot, she would never say who the father was. There was a good reason for this. She told friends that she had become pregnant by 'immaculate conception' following a mystical experience at Stonehenge. By whatever means she had become pregnant Sheena saw in the baby she was carrying a strange link to 'other worlds' beyond our own.

So when the baby was born on 9 May 1983 Sheena called her Kether Boleskine, names that echoed mystic and occult symbolism. Kether was an aspect of the 'Tree of Life', a mystical chart dating from the time of the Egyptians and used by black magicians and witches to conjure up the spirits of the dead. She gave her baby the middle name 'Boleskine' in honour of an infamous site on the shores of Loch Ness. The country house in which Satanist Aleister Crowley carried out magical rites to make contact with demons from other dimensions.

Although he was not Kether's father Alan Jeffrey Porter (24), born and brought up in the Gorbals, moved into a Maryhill flat with Sheena and Kether in August 1983. Porter, a painter and decorator, shared Sheena's obsession with the 'other side'. He was a practising spiritualist who attended a church in Anderston. Porter was also a 'channeller', a psychic who had the ability to 'bring over' healing energy from other dimensions and he used this ability to help people who came to him with ailments.

But what was going on between Porter and McLaughlan over the summer of 1983 when they were living together? What was the driving force that led to a bizarre and abnormal act being perpetrated? During the night of 26 August 1983 Alan Porter and Sheena McLaughlan walked from Glasgow to Balloch Castle country park on the shores of Loch Lomond. Little Kether, now three months old, was with them: she was in her pram and, quite amazingly, was pushed the entire twenty miles by Porter and McLaughlan. They stopped at an isolated spot called Stablewood, beside a shingle beach.

Although both Porter and McLaughlan agreed on the night's events up to that point they gave different versions of what happened next. Sheena claimed that Porter had drugged her and when they reached Loch Lomond she went for a walk alone leaving Kether with him. When she returned the baby was dead. But Porter offered a more bizarre account, which, at least on the face of it, was in keeping with the couple's interest in the occult. Porter claimed that, although he had real psychic ability, Sheena occupied a higher spiritual plane and he was under her control. He described her as 'like an angel' and explained that she had told him that 'a spiritual force was guiding her'. He claimed McLaughlan was insisting that, 'The baby had to die.'

If his account is true it is not clear, however, why Sheena believed the baby's death to be necessary. It was her Tibetan spirit guide, it seems, who first warned McLaughlan that baby Kether could pose a threat of some kind and who first warned her, 'Your baby has to die.' Sheena claimed, 'I kept getting these visions. I kept seeing my baby's head covered in blood.' There seems little doubt that McLaughlan was being driven by her 'guide' to end the life of Kether Boleskine. But it was never clear whether the threat was personal against McLaughlan herself and the baby's father or was a wider one. Did McLaughlan see in Kether an image of the Devil, or one of his legion of demons? The evidence suggests that at the very least McLaughlan believed that in Kether's conception some kind of paranormal or occult force had been involved. And that the power involved in the baby's conception had been of the darker kind.

Sheena, however, though she later blamed Porter, lied at the time about Kether's fate, telling her mother, Mrs Flora McLaughlan, that the baby was staying with her father. Later she claimed to friends that she was making a pop record and that Kether had died of cancer. Meanwhile, she and Porter travelled down to Brighton where they spent some time, but, unable to settle, were soon on the move again, staying in North Uist before returning to Glasgow. By May 1984, when Kether would have been a year old, Sheena had split from Porter and moved in with a new boyfriend, William, at a caravan site in Errogie, Inverness-shire. By a strange twist of fate it was just a few miles from infamous Boleskine House at Loch Ness, after which Kether had been given her middle name. Sheena now confessed to a horrified William that she had killed Kether. She returned to the site of the crime and claimed to feel baby Kether's spirit 'all around her'.

But Sheena could never keep up a relationship for long and was soon back in Maryhill, still concealing the truth about Kether's death. It was not till August 1985, two years after the event, that she broke down and confessed to her parents that Kether had been killed and left on Loch Lomond-side. The police were immediately involved and traced Alan Porter to Hove near Brighton. He admitted his involvement in Kether's death, though he put the blame on Sheena, claiming: 'It was a spiritual thing. It was not us. It was a spiritual force.'

McLaughlan took police to the spot where, she said, the baby had died. Although a few baby items were discovered there was no sign of little Kether's remains. Alan Porter, meanwhile, claimed that he had put an end to Kether as a 'mercy killing', after Sheena had tried but failed to choke the baby to death. He had then wrapped Kether's body in a pink blanket and placed the bundle beside a burn. He alleged that immediately after he had murdered

Kether, Sheena had wanted to have sexual intercourse in the woods. A sex act would certainly be in keeping with magic ritual. Practitioners of the 'black arts' believe that sex and death can generate powerful mystic forces. However, according to Porter, he had refused to take part and as Sheena denied asking for sex there's no way of being sure of just what was intended.

Although McLaughlan and Porter gave different versions of how Kether died, both were convicted at Glasgow High Court in January 1986. Sheena admitted culpable homicide and, in February 1986, was sentenced to five years. The presiding judge Lord Wyllie commented, 'This young woman does not appear to have any remorse. She still maintains she is in touch with the spirit world and that holy men are walking beside her. It would appear that she is still involved in the spirit world and thinks that the child is content.' Porter, found guilty of murder, received a life sentence. It will come as no surprise to learn that the courts weren't interested in any supernatural explanation of Kether's death. So the question was never answered of who exactly was Sheena's spirit guide, what his motives were and whether strange rituals might have been carried out as Kether died. Nor was any attempt made to consider whether an evil entity from another dimension might somehow have set out to control events and engineer a tragic end. So can the death of Kether be explained simply as the sad consequence of the bizarre workings of a troubled mind?

The sudden descent of Philip Givens into murder may suggest otherwise. To friends and relatives Phil Givens appeared perfectly harmless. His sister Margaret described him as 'such a kindly man. He used to bring home injured birds and stray cats and dogs. Almost every spare penny he had went on them. He never smoked or drank. That's one of the reasons we never thought there was the slightest bit of harm in him.' In 1962 Phil Givens had reached the age of thirty-five and held down a steady, well-paid job as a garage mechanic. He was even planning to emigrate to Canada to make a better life for himself and was gathering the necessary documentation to apply. But almost overnight the 'harmless' part of Philip Givens's character disappeared. In the quiet of his bedroom Phil Givens started to hear voices. Evil voices which appeared to be coming from another dimension. One voice in particular claimed to be that of the Devil and urged Givens to abduct and murder young men. Givens found the voice of the invisible entity impossible to resist. Whatever it was that was communicating with him, Givens found that it was exercising more and more control over his life.

In July 1962 sixteen-year-old Philip Martin, an apprentice slater who had been sent on an errand, was walking along Clydebank's Glasgow Road when a small black car drew up alongside. The driver, who was wearing a navy-blue donkey jacket with a checked cap, offered Philip ten shillings to help to move a fireplace. Philip got into the car and was driven to a derelict shop at 89 Stobcross Street in the Anderston district of Glasgow. Philip Martin described what happened next:

> A grate was lying in the back shop, pulled out from the wall. It was very dark and the man lit a candle. Suddenly he poked a gun in my ribs and told me to stand by the wall. I laughed at first hoping it was a joke, but it wasn't. The man made me strip, threw me on a chair and tied me up. I thought I was going to die. He gagged me with adhesive tape. Then he snuffed out the candle and left. I managed to bump my way into the front shop and I was getting the gag off when the man came in.

Unfortunately for Philip Martin the entity who was instructing Givens in the art of violence, the 'Devil', had warned Givens that Martin had broken free and had ordered him to go back to bind him more tightly. Givens tied Philip up again, making sure that he was secure, then left. There's little doubt that Givens intended to return, to suffocate and most probably abuse him and that this was his intention from the start. Luckily for Philip Martin his cries for help were heard in the house next door and he was set free. His horrifying ordeal seemed to show that though the voices contacting Givens were not all-seeing, they were certainly determined to make sure that Givens carried out whatever 'master plan' they envisaged. Or had these events simply sprung from the inner workings of Givens's perverted mind? Whatever the true cause a tragic outcome was inevitable.

On 3 October 1962 a sanitary inspector, Malcolm Beaton, was called to a disused surgery at 66 West Bridgend in Dumbarton, following a neighbour's report of a foul smell coming from the premises. He brought a joiner, Bruce McColl, with him, to force open the locked door. Inside, the shocked pair discovered the near-naked body of a young man; it was strapped to a chair with a gag across the mouth. His hands and legs had been bound with bootlaces and insulating tape. His ankles had been tied to the iron supports of a sink. The body had been partly burned. The corpse was soon identified as that of Frederick Dowden, aged fifteen. From the decomposed state of the torso it seemed clear that Frederick had lain there for some time and had probably been killed soon after he had gone missing on 7 August. However, forensic examination revealed no obvious signs of injuries. A likely explanation was that Frederick had slowly suffocated during a prolonged assault by the attacker, during which ropes were pulled ever more tightly round his chest. The fact that he had been stripped of clothing, bound and left in empty premises reminded detectives of the Philip Martin case. An incident that was still under investigation.

The police were aware that these were no spur-of-the-moment crimes, but carefully thought through by the man responsible. The killer having first spent time identifying empty shops then contacted the owner in order to view them to make sure they fitted his requirements. For the empty surgery where Fred Dowden met his death the killer had paid two months rent in advance and given a false address in Dumbarton. He had then painted over windows with black paint so that it was dark inside and hidden from passers-by. He even went to the extent of buying second-hand chairs of the kind he believed would be more suited to his assault on his teenage victims. Some of this detectives learned from their inquiries. The full picture would only emerge after they identified the killer. It was a clever and calculated plan. One which, on the face of it, the mild-mannered, respectable Givens would never have carried out. It was almost as if another being had entered into his mind and body and was directing his life.

Police were convinced that they had a potential serial killer on their hands, one driven by dark forces. And they were so concerned that there might be more deaths that for the first time an identikit picture of the attacker was broadcast on television. On the evening that the identikit was broadcast, Phil Givens was sitting in his home at Ardenlea Street, Dalmarnock in Glasgow. His sister later described the scene, 'When the identikit picture of Phil flashed on the TV screen, he was sitting with my son and daughter. My daughter said, "There's the man that the police are after." Phil joked that he was the man they wanted. We never believed it for a second.' Perhaps in his mind Phil Givens believed he was innocent of the crime. That it was the Devil – whom he was powerless to resist, and kept urging him to horrific acts of violence – who was really responsible for these terrible events.

Top psychologists were asked to construct a character profile of Frederick's killer. In their view, the murderer would be over thirty, unmarried and living with his mother. A remarkably accurate assessment. In fact, the killer's sister had become a substitute 'mum', whom he lived with after his mother's death. But, in reality, it was solid detective work that nailed Givens. It was known that the attacker used an old, black car which police thought was a 1950 Ford Anglia. When detective constable Cameron Wiseman arrived at the home of the sixteenth owner of this type of vehicle on his list the man explained that he had been in Canada over the period of the murder of Fred Dowden. Wiseman then learned that the car had been lent to a friend during this time. The friend's name was Phil Givens. Wiseman went to the garage where Givens worked as a mechanic and was struck immediately by the similarity between the description of the attacker provided by Philip Martin and Givens. Fingerprint comparison proved that Phil Givens was the man they had been looking for.

At his trial in March 1963, psychiatric evidence was presented that claimed to show Givens sought sexual pleasure from putting into practice his fantasy of tying up young men. The court's recommendation was that Givens be confined in a state mental hospital without a time limit. The trial judge, Lord Mackintosh, told Givens, 'I hold that you being a person of dangerous, violent and criminal propensity require treatment under conditions of special security.' Even the experts were forced to admit that Givens was beyond help. So what had turned mild-mannered Givens into a murderer?

One aspect that was never considered was the reality of the satanic voice that Givens claimed had urged him to attack and kill. It might be asked why, if Givens was a psychiatric case who was beyond help, he managed to hold down a demanding job as a car mechanic and appear so completely normal. Could it be true that the Devil himself, or one of his demons, had managed to take over Givens's life?

Death itself, psychics claim, releases energy forces that can be used by black magicians and to sustain demons, the 'other world' servants of the Devil. A prolonged death, such as that suffered by Givens's victim, can increase tenfold the power of the energy released. There had also been an attempt to set Fred Dowden alight and fire is recognised in mystic circles as the generator of powerful occult forces. And, on top of that, there was a clear sexual aspect to the case. It's well known that the Devil sets out to exploit any sexual weakness in those he is seeking to control. Violent death coupled with a sexual element seems to generate even more powerful forces than death alone. Or so practitioners of the black arts believe. From across the world cases are reported of individuals who claim that some outside force of evil, known as the Devil, encouraged them to acts of wickedness. No doubt some may be mentally disturbed, but can this be true of every case? Do we simply stick on a label because it is convenient and allows us to avoid facing up to the disturbing possibility that the Devil and his demons might, in fact, exist? It must be wondered why, given such a dramatic change in character, Philip Givens, who had reached the age of thirty-five, had never shown evidence of bizarre traits before so abruptly transforming into a vicious killer. Did it take a paranormal event, the appearance of the real Devil, to change his behaviour? On the other hand, it might be asked why, if Givens was under his control, Satan did not save him when he had warned him on other occasions. That, however, is to misunderstand the aims of the Devil. As his followers have testified, Satan and his demons like nothing more than to lead people into evil acts and then abandon them. It's a bizarre game, but one with a purpose that benefits only the Devil. And he always seems to find victims willing to play along.

Often murders appear, on the face of it, motiveless. Or at least there appears no obvious cause such as jealousy, hate or straight-forward robbery. So what gets into a man's mind and makes him a killer? What demon drives him to commit the most horrific crime of all? Is there evidence, as in the case of Phil Givens, that a sudden, inexplicable, character change can take place? One that turns an apparently harmless, or even loving, individual into a cold, calculating assassin? At first glance, Iain Scoular surely fits the bill.

Scoular was certainly no angel or high flier even though his father, John, was a successful businessman and the family lived in an expensive private development in Cambuslang. But despite his background Iain was a boy with problems. At school he was described as immature, and tended to hang around with children younger than himself. He also told lies constantly and was referred to a psychiatrist as a result. Although his parents had high hopes for him he left Cathkin High School with one 'O' grade, in wood-work, and eventually found a job as a forklift-truck driver. Much of his social life centred around visiting pubs, where he frittered away large sums of money on fruit machines. Indeed he became so obsessed with gambling that he would hand over his pay packet to his father on a Friday night to limit his spending. Despite his apparent lack of interest in girls, he met, and fell in love with, a young woman in a local club in July 1980, when he was twenty-two. The object of his affection described Scoular as, 'the perfect gentleman . . . he was never pushy or fresh and did not try to have sex with me'. Ignoring the disapproval of Scoular's parents about her modest background – she was brought up in a council house and worked in a factory – the couple got engaged. Although he was an adult Scoular's mother still kept a protective eye on him. She admitted to 'old-fashioned views' on the family and would wait up for her son and daughter if they were out for the evening.

Iain Scoular was never going to set the world alight, but his life was not a complete dead end. He had devoted parents, a loving fiancée, held down a job and was far from being on the bread line. And there was no evidence that he was capable of horrific acts of violence. But in the autumn of 1982 that was to change abruptly.

The detectives who found the body at three o'clock on the morning of 1 October 1982 knew they were dealing with a brutal killer. Catherine McChord, a thirty-six-year-old taxi driver from Carmyle, had been stabbed twice in the head and three times through her breasts. Her killer had then stuffed the corpse into the luggage compartment of her cab, where it lay on Braeside Place, Cambuslang till police, alerted by Catherine's disappearance, arrived on the scene. Catherine had met a violent end, but there had been clearly something else going through the killer's mind. Before leaving the scene he had, in a bizarre twist, laid out Catherine's ignition key, inhaler and cigarette lighter in a straight line on the driver's seat, an action reminiscent of the ritual killer. Police also came to the conclusion that the killer, in a weird act of risk-taking, had spent an hour alone in the taxi with Catherine's body. It was not clear, however, what, if anything, had occurred during this time.

Police soon discovered that the victim had a criminal conviction. Catherine had been found guilty of a £143,500 fraud involving a Spot the Ball competition in the *Scottish Daily Express* and sentenced to three years in prison. So had she been the victim of an underworld hit? This line of inquiry soon petered out. Catherine's murder appeared motiveless. But a random killing sent alarm bells ringing. To detectives it signalled that the perpetrator was likely to strike again.

Appeals were published in local newspapers asking witnesses to come forward. A taxi like the one driven by Mrs McChord was parked in areas she had worked in to jog memories. In fact a number of people did remember seeing her the night she died. She was a conspicuous figure, always immaculately dressed, loaded down with jewellery and wearing an elaborate wig. Yet police were nevertheless disappointed by the response, and some officers attributed this to the victim's conviction for fraud. As time went on the number of officers involved fell as leads were exhausted. But the men in charge of the investigation knew that it was only a matter of time before the killer struck again.

Elizabeth Walton was a nursing sister who lived in the Cambuslang area with her husband and children. After a night-out in Glasgow with a female friend to celebrate her recovery from illness, Mrs Walton made her way home by train arriving at Cambuslang station just after eleven. Her normal practice was to phone home for a lift but this time she decided to walk to her house, which was less than half a mile away. She never reached her destination. She was knocked unconscious then dragged into thick undergrowth next to West Coats primary school – the very school attended by her nine-year-old daughter. Here she was strangled and savagely beaten. When she was dead the killer stripped her of her clothing then mutilated the body with a knife. Still not content with his handiwork he then 'decorated' his victim by slashing her wrists and cutting her thighs. The killer also tied her clothes in knots.

It was a sadistic murder, but the ritual marks made by the killer raised questions about his motives. Could this have been some kind of bizarre offering? In ancient times victims would be 'decorated' with cut marks and killed to appease the gods. In more recent times sacrificial victims in black-magic rites, it has been alleged, are slashed or marked with signs which satisfy the desire of the demonic elements the black magician is attempting to conjure up. Where the occult and murder come together there always appears to be a ritual involved. It's as if the ritual somehow transforms the act into a power or force the denizens of the 'other side' can use. But what makes a murder a ritual killing? It must be carried out for a reason other than the perverted pleasure of depriving another human being of life. To those involved in the dark side of magic the act of death has a special significance releasing, they believe, a form of energy which can be used for other, maybe demonic, purposes.

Seventy-two hours after Mrs Walton was killed a local man contacted police with information that could potentially crack the case. The witness, Iain Scoular, aged twenty-four, was personable and well dressed. Police quickly learned that he came from a respectable family. He told detectives that at about 11 p.m. on 2 December 1982 he had been walking home from the pub when he saw a strange man acting suspiciously near the spot where Elizabeth Walton had been murdered. At the time, he said, he thought little of it and went straight home. The officer in charge instructed officers to follow this up by checking out the lead and – given that Scoular had been in the vicinity of the crime scene around the time of the murder – detectives spoke to those who knew him well. It was at this stage that police discovered there was more to Scoular than could be guessed at first glance.

They questioned him repeatedly over an eight-week period, and noted gaps in his story. But it was information inadvertently provided by Jean Scoular that helped to seal her son's fate. She told detectives that he had not returned home until one o'clock on the night of

Elizabeth Walton's murder. Indeed she remembered the time clearly because she had been out looking for Iain and they had a heated argument about him being out so late. Scoular, on the other hand, had told police that he arrived home shortly after eleven.

Exposed as a liar Scoular desperately changed his story. He claimed that he had not gone home at eleven but had visited a friend's house to watch a video; police discovered this was also a lie. His next claim was that he had crossed the road to avoid the 'suspicious stranger', who, he said, scared him and had then gone to a local park to sober up. This seemed unlikely because, if he was afraid, why go to a park late at night where he could have been mugged? With a definite suspect, police could now explore other avenues. There was not only scientific evidence linking Scoular to the crime scenes but also witnesses were found who identified Scoular as the man seen running at full pelt through Cambuslang shopping centre not long after the murder.

Although detectives were unsure if there was a connection between the McChord and Walton murders an interview with Scoular's mother helped to change their minds. Jean Scoular first threatened to walk out after being grilled by detectives and then made a statement that implicated her son in the death of Catherine McChord. 'It's a wonder you are not blaming him for the taxi murder. It's as well he was at home with his father and I that night.' This was at odds with Scoular's version of events, which was already under threat from two witnesses who identified him as the man they had seen running away from her taxi. It was also established that Mrs McChord had been stabbed by a left hander and Scoular was left handed. And it was surely no coincidence that Scoular lived only a few hundred yards from the scene of both murders.

The trial of Iain Scoular for the murders of Catherine McChord and Elizabeth Walton began at the end of May 1983. He pleaded not guilty and lodged a special defence of alibi in both cases. During the trial the jury heard a mass of evidence and were shown horrific photographs of Mrs Walton's naked body. The proceedings had no visible effect on Scoular, who exhibited a complete lack of emotion. This was in tune with his behaviour when being interrogated by police, who noted that he was always polite, helpful and calm. In fact, on one occasion he even halved his sandwich and offered it to the startled officer sitting across the desk. The only time he lost his cool was during questioning by the prosecution about his sexual inadequacies. Psychiatrists who had examined him came to the conclusion that, as well as being a psychopath, he was impotent.

While the jury members were considering their verdict, Scoular sat alone in his cell reading a novel, apparently without a care in the world. When he returned to the dock he again showed no emotion as the jury brought in a guilty verdict on both charges. He even nonchalantly popped a sweet into his mouth as the verdicts were being read out. The judge, Lord Allanbridge, handed down life sentences for both murders, with a recommendation that Scoular should serve at least twenty years.

The ritualistic manner in which Scoular dealt with the bodies of his victims suggests that strange forces were at work in his mind. Occult forces? Or simply a man possessed by abnormal thoughts? Or can evil from a world outside our own enter a man's soul and transform him into a vicious killing machine? A murderer might not even be aware of his sudden change of character; he might not realise that he is being used by others for a dark purpose. But other killers do appear to have a clear motive for their deeds. There are, undoubtedly, ritual murders which take place with a very definite end in view.

To achieve their ends how far are people willing to go to create a powerful magic spell? The evidence is that some are prepared to descend into the very depths of evil. Was this the motive behind the Bible John killings? Serial murders from the 1960s that shocked a nation and remain unsolved to this day.

By the time the man who became known as 'Bible John' turned

up at Glasgow's Barrowland ballroom that Saturday in August 1969 he had already killed once. In February 1968 he had been prowling the same dance hall and struck up a conversation with twenty-five-year-old Patricia Docker. Witnesses saw the couple at various times as John walked Patricia back to her home in Langside Place. At some point in the early hours of the following morning, Friday, 23 February, John strangled Patricia and left her unclothed body in Carmichael Place just round the corner from where she stayed. She had been having her period and John had deliberately removed the sanitary towel she was wearing. It seemed an odd thing to do, even surprising experienced police officers who had seen more than their fair share of strange behaviour. The police jumped to the conclusion that the killer had been frustrated in his attempts to have intercourse and his 'passion' had turned to murder. Oddly, in spite of the fact that both John and Patricia had met at a busy venue no one remembered seeing them. There was a good reason for this. The police believed that Pat had attended the Majestic ballroom in Hope Street. They spent a fruitless two weeks interviewing patrons at the dance hall before someone tipped them off that she must have met John at the Barrowland. The place she had actually gone to though not set out for. By the time they discovered their mistake the trail for the killer had gone cold.

Not that John cared. He took incredible risks to get what he wanted. Even turning up at a dance hall on a Saturday night was taking a chance. In spite of the heaving crowd, if you were chatting to one of the women, you might easily be remembered by her pal. But John didn't seem to worry too much. He'd already chosen one victim from the same dance hall. Now Jemima McDonald, a single mother of three, was unfortunate enough to be the next. Exactly why or how she got into conversation with John is unknown. But around midnight Mima left the Barrowland and set off for her tenement address in Mackeith Street. She wasn't alone. She felt safe enough in John's company to allow him to walk her back to her flat.

Several hours later, on the morning of Saturday, 17 August, Mima's body was discovered by her sister Margaret in a derelict building only thirty yards from her home. Police quickly noticed similarities with the murder of Patricia Docker some eighteen months before. Both had last been seen alive in the company of a man they had met at the Barrowland. Both women had been strangled and their handbags had been stolen. They had been having their period and the murderer had carefully removed each woman's sanitary towel. It all seemed more than coincidence.

Witnesses soon came forward claiming to have seen Mima. They had caught a good view of her companion. He was quite a distinctive individual. To the police it seemed that if his picture could be widely displayed, someone somewhere would be bound to recognise him. It duly appeared with a volley of publicity and a detailed description of 'John'. He was, the public were told, 'aged 25–35. 6 feet to 6 feet 2 inches tall. Slim build with a thin pale face. He had reddish fair hair, cut short and brushed back. He was wearing a blue suit of good quality with hand-stitched lapels and a white shirt.'

But John seemed relaxed about the intense media interest. He carried on as if he was from another world, not even bothering to change the venue at which he selected his victims. There were dozens of dance halls in 1960s Glasgow, but John headed straight back to the Barrowland for his final killing day.

As he moved through the crowd, he seemed almost indifferent to the picture he presented. According to Jean Langford he stood out from the men who usually turned up. Smartly dressed though he undoubtedly was his clothes had little in common with Sixties fashion. She chuckled at his well-tailored brown suit with three buttons, the blue shirt and diagonally striped tie. John's cutaway suede boots caused Jean real amusement and she overheard one of the dancers make a joke about them. Jean had made the trip to the Barrowland that Thursday with her sister Helen Puttock. They both enjoyed dancing and though Helen was married her husband had no objection to her evening out. And so Helen struck up a conversation with John while Jean danced with another man who also gave his name as 'John'. Neither sister's dancing partner claimed to know the other.

Did John have murder on his mind at this stage? Commonsense would indicate that he did not. Not only had he allowed himself to be seen closely by two people he had no intention of killing but also as the two couples left the dance hall John demanded to see the manager. The cigarette machine in the foyer had jammed when Helen tried to buy a packet. According to Jean, John became enraged and complained to the manager and then to the assistant manager. He could hardly fail to notice that he was drawing attention to himself.

But he seemed unconcerned and even then he didn't steal away into the night, but calmly walked down the road with Jean, Helen and 'John' to the taxi rank where they waited and chatted till a cab was free. Now they were down to three as the other John waved goodbye and headed for a bus. He was never heard from again. Bible John, Helen and Jean clambered into the taxi. Now there was another potential witness. The taxi driver. As it turned out he couldn't remember much about his passengers, but John could hardly have guessed that when he got into his cab. John, as can be imagined, had more important matters on his mind. He was anxious to get Helen on her own so told the cabman to let Jean off first even though she lived further down the road than her sister.

Jean was dropped off at the Kelso Street roundabout, waved goodbye to Helen, and watched the taxi turn back towards Earl Street, Helen's address. A short while later the cab stopped to let John and Helen out. They must have quickly headed for a back court not far from Helen's flat. By one o' clock Helen was dead and not a soul had heard her cry out. She was found lying face down in the back court where she had led John. She still had on the ocelot fur coat and black woollen dress she had worn on the previous night's trip to the Barrowland. But it was clear from the grass on her body and marks on the ground that Helen had made a frantic attempt to escape when John began his attack. Like Patricia and Jemima before her she had been strangled and sexually assaulted.

The sisters' journey in the taxi, where Jean had spoken with John, now became of key importance. The killer had given clues about himself, but how far could they be relied upon? It was on this final journey that John made reference to his knowledge of the Bible and was dubbed by the press Bible John. He quoted passages although it wasn't necessarily clear from which part of the Old or New Testament they came. There seemed to be a reference to the story of Moses among the bulrushes. But knowledge of that famous incident, often taught in schools, hardly requires a Biblical scholar.

It was also during the taxi ride that Jean believed she heard John mutter something about his surname. She didn't quite catch what he said and thought it sounded like Templeton, Sempleton or Emerson. They do have a similar sound, but Jean's memory could well be hazy on the matter because if John mentioned all three he was clearly not referring to a surname. Could he have been saying something completely different? Something that does have a biblical connection. What he may have actually muttered was not 'Templeton, Sempleton, Emerson', but the 'Temple of Solomon, Jerusalem'. It would also link with John's reference to Moses. It was Moses who led the Jewish people out of slavery in Egypt. He had with him the mystical Ark of the Covenant, a strange box-like structure built under God's direct instruction. The Ark was eventually housed within the Temple of Solomon in Jerusalem. The site of the Temple was regarded even in Western Europe as one where strange, paranormal events could occur. In the twelfth century the first leaders of the mysterious Knights Templar organisation dug into the then ruined Temple and removed various objects they discovered. Objects that were believed to possess supernatural power. Some of these artefacts, it is claimed, ended up in Scotland when the Templars fled to this country to escape accusations of devil worship. True or not there can be no doubting that the Templars inspired a whole range of secret societies from the Freemasons to more arcane practitioners of the Black Arts. Even today, there are individuals who believe they possess secret knowledge and that by using certain materials, phrases and rituals they can gain access to hidden worlds denied to most of us. Could Bible John have been one of them?

There is one common thread in the Bible John murders: all three women were having their monthly period at the time John met and then strangled them. Did he know that for Patricia, Mima and Helen this was 'that time' of the month? Or was it pure 'bad luck' for the victims? The police held the view that if John had been allowed by the women a certain amount of sexual intimacy, then the murders would not have occurred. In other words, John, his sexual urges aroused, found that his female companions would not allow him to go any further. John's response, the police believed, was either one of sexual disgust or fury.

But how could John have guessed when he met them that Patricia, Mima and Helen were having a period? The odds against picking up three women, one after the other, each of whom is in that bodily state, would make it a highly unlikely sequence. However, if John was only attacking women who aroused his loathing he must have picked up several women before and during the period June 1967 to October 1969. Women he had a normal relationship with, but who have never come forward. So what triggered the explosion when he encountered a woman who was having a period? Was it some perverse, twisted desire to force an outlet for the violence contained within him?

Or did he have a more definite purpose in mind? Did Bible John deliberately target women having a period for a sinister, but not sexual, purpose? It is possible that far from being frustrated by the fact that his female friends were having a period, John was looking to collect their blood. Menstrual blood, though it may seem difficult to believe, was regarded as possessing magical properties by a wide variety of magic-obsessed cults. In his book *Spells, Curses and Magical Recipes*, Leonard Ashley writes, 'Some witches were thought to sign pacts with the Devil in menstrual blood.' Blood in itself is an important and very potent ingredient of ritual magic: blood from a virgin or a menstruating woman possesses even greater power. It is possible that John believed his victim's blood flow to have supernatural properties. Could John then have been part of some strange black-magic group? One to which menstrual blood formed a significant ritual object.

Unlikely? In each case the sanitary towel that the victim was using was carefully removed and in Helen Puttock's case, the final murder, placed beneath the left armpit as if left as a clue. A hint the killer guessed the police would never understand. And an act that does not suggest a man who was disgusted or angered by encountering a woman who was having a period. It would suggest that far from repulsing him, it was what he had come for. It was this realisation that may have triggered the panic evident in Helen Puttock's desperate attempts to escape. Attempts that, strangely, went unnoticed even though the murder took place, according to the police, at the back of a close.

Serial killers do not stop because they have found something more 'interesting' to do. They don't suddenly decide to take up darts because they've had enough of murder. They keep going till they get caught or they die. But serial murder with a purpose is a different story. 'John' stopped because he had got what he wanted. And if he was involved with others, it may be that he had obtained for them what they wanted. However, John could well have been acting on his own. A psychological profile of Bible John indicated that he would be the type of person who would have an active interest in black magic and the occult. It could well be that such an obsession drove him to commit murder with no help from anyone.

But if he was a man driven by obsession why did he slip away so abruptly and so successfully? Because, after Helen Puttock's murder, he disappeared as though he had never been. The man we remember as Bible John seems to have known that like a phantom he could vanish into the night and never be seen again.

So was there a cover up? If so, that would have to involve the police and suggest that officers were involved in occult circles of some kind. That seems highly unlikely. But if there was a plan to target specific women then John could well have had accomplices. Jean Langford remarked on the length of time both her own and Helen's John spent together in the male toilets as they got ready to go. Clearly, a conversation was going on. And it was highly convenient that, as Bible John was getting into conversation with Helen, the second John was engaging Jean's attention. Then, at the last moment, as they wait at the taxi rank, Jean's partner walks off for a bus, leaving Bible John to travel with the two women, knowing that at some point he and Helen will be left on their own. In fact, Jean's John shares a key fate with Bible John. After 31 October neither is ever seen or heard of again.

31 October. The day on which Helen's body was found. An important day in the occult calendar. The day on which the veil between this world and the next is at its thinnest. It's the best day in the year, black magicians believe, on which to summon up the spirits of the dead. But it could, of course, just be coincidence. As may be the fact that there were three victims. Three is one of the most powerful mystical numbers. And to practitioners of black magic, numbers bring influence especially over entities from other worlds. They are also highly symbolic. So, to a twisted mind, to kill three women, the last on 31 October, would be in occult terms a highly significant act. One that could raise the perpetrator's ability to greater levels in ritual magic. So Bible John's killing spree could have come to an end because he had achieved what he set out to do. And there was simply no need to carry on and run the risk again of being caught.